ROOTS OF THE REPUBLIC

Roots of the Republic

A New Perspective
on Early American Constitutionalism

GEORGE DARGO

PRAEGER PUBLISHERS
New York • Washington

For
Lois,
Jessica,
and
Stephen

Published in the United States of America in 1974
by Praeger Publishers, Inc.
111 Fourth Avenue, New York, N.Y. 10003

© 1974 by Praeger Publishers, Inc.

Library of Congress Cataloging in Publication Data

Dargo, George.
  Roots of the Republic.

  (New perspectives in American history)
  Bibliography: p. 159.
  1. United States—Politics and government—Colonial period. 2. United
States—Constitutional history. I. Title.
JK54.D35   320.9′73′02   74-118049

Printed in the United States of America

Acknowledgments

I welcome this opportunity to thank James Shenton, not only for his enthusiastic interest in this book, but for having encouraged me to pursue the study of history, United States history in particular, in the days when I was an undergraduate at Columbia College.

I also want to thank the staff at Praeger for their excellent and efficient work at every stage of production. Gladys Topkis's unerring editorial judgment and keen sense of style made this a much better book than it otherwise would have been.

I also wish to express my gratitude to colleagues at City College. Robert Hajdu read a very early draft of this work and made a number of invaluable suggestions regarding material pertinent to Chapters 1 and 4. I am indebted to Oscar Zeichner for his careful reading of the manuscript in more finished form. I benefited, too, from the advice of Michael Weisser and Emanuel Chill on particular points. Alan Gardner, now a graduate student at Columbia, rendered excellent research assistance in assembling some of the bibliographical data. Needless to say, any errors of fact or weaknesses of interpretation that remain are my own responsibility.

Contents

Foreword

by James P. Shenton

Nothing in history is fixed in its interpretation. The historian is forever re-examining evidence or examining new evidence to develop new understandings of past events. As his awareness of the complexity of the human condition and of its social expression deepens, the historian struggles to incorporate these added dimensions within his discipline.

The process of historical reinterpretation, which adds excitement to the task of being a historian, in some measure is a reflection of the changing needs and interests of new generations. More fundamentally, new interpretations of history reflect the profound forces that operate to bring about social change. For the historian, like any other man, is not immune to the influence of the currents that shape the experience and attitudes of his time.

In the decades since the end of World War II, historians have increasingly employed the tools and techniques of analysis developed by sociologists, political scientists, social psychologists, and anthropologists. Armed with these interdisciplinary methods, they have been better equipped to probe the complex motivations of men. Their ability to analyze the extraordinary variety of mass behavior has been vastly improved by the use of statistical analysis and computers to unravel the meaning of mountains of raw data. It now seems possible to explain not only the behavior of a handful of people but that of whole cities, classes, and even societies.

More important than the changes in methodology are the changes in historians' attitudes and approaches, reflecting the impact of vast social changes. Thus, for example, the black revolution in America and abroad has obliged historians to abandon their traditional preoccupation with governing elites to examine the interaction of whites and blacks on all levels of human experience. Americans have suddenly become aware that a vast segment of their national life, that of nonwhites, has been shrouded in neglect. And, because so much of the nonwhite experience has been that of a downtrodden and oppressed people, historians have had to begin to develop techniques of analysis that will permit an understanding of how the common man functioned. In a world growing smaller, a world in which the masses of mankind aspire to a fuller dignity, historians are faced with the demand that they probe the history of the many rather than the few. To meet this demand, they are beginning to explore not only the history of nonwhites but also that of the neglected female. Similarly, historians are beginning to look into the ways in which ethnic origin has affected American whites—for example, the attitudes and behavior of American labor.

With the new effort to understand the individual in mass society has come a desire to know more about the functioning of the institutions that affect everyman. The family, the school, the system of criminal justice, the institutions of government, to name but a few, are being subjected to deepening scrutiny by historians as well as other social scientists.

The authors of this series, well aware of these significant changes in the world and in historians' way of interpreting it, are attempting a twofold task. They seek, first, to synthesize the most recent scholarship on a significant period or theme in American history. Second, they attempt to project contemporary relevance into past experience so as to give the student a fresh perspective on material that may be familiar to him in more conventional presentation. The consistent emphasis on changing interpretations, it is hoped, will stimulate interest in history as a dynamic discipline and will dispel any lingering vestiges of the myth that historians are somehow above the fray, uniquely capable of pure objectivity.

No aspect of the American political system is more distinctive than the insistence on written constitutional guarantees. The origin of this singularly American preoccupation is the subject that Professor Dargo explores in this book. In it he demonstrates that the American emphasis on these constitutional definitions of the outermost limits of legitimate authority is rooted in the earliest period of American history, and even before, in the history of England.

American constitutional guarantees have served as profoundly conservative inhibitions on the holders of political power. In a fundamental sense, they preserve Americans from the unrestrained exercise of sovereignty. They are sentinels standing watch against the development of absolute, unchecked power and offering assurance that individual liberties will not be overwhelmed by the pretensions of aggressive authority.

ROOTS OF THE REPUBLIC

1

Introduction: Constitutionalism in the American Experience

The United States is the laboratory for Western constitutionalism. From its early colonial origins through the period of constitutional formation and on into the nineteenth century, American government has always been on the cutting edge of political modernization. A blend of antecedent European models plus indigenous growths born of necessity, inventiveness, and a willingness to experiment, American government has been admired around the world for its enlightened liberalism. If, in our own time, the American constitutional system appears to be frozen in the mold of the past, we need only look back into our now ancient constitutional traditions to recognize that interest in new ideas about government has always been our forte and aptitude for change our abiding strength.

Constitutionalism is a very old concept—perhaps as old as government itself. It is rooted in a simple idea: that power requires restraint. In different periods of history, such restraint has assumed varied forms. In Europe during the Middle Ages, for example, restraint was built into the very fabric of the social order. Power was diffused. The state was embodied in the person of the monarch, but princes were merely first among equals. Their power was held in check by the countervailing pressures of the great nobility, the high clergy, corporate bodies, universities, towns, professions, and privileged orders. Men talked of "liberties" rather than of Liberty. They claimed "privileges," "immunities," and "franchises" guaranteed to them in law. These words described rights to perform or not to perform prescribed services or obligations and served as standing acknowledgment of the power that the parties claiming them possessed. In other words, liberties were not the safeguard of the powerless against the powerful. Rather, they defined the boundaries separating one powerful social entity from another. Power was requisite to liberty, and the wide dispersion of liberties served to check the concentration of power.

What stands between Western medieval and modern constitutionalism is the prolonged convulsion through which much of Europe passed from the fifteenth through the seventeenth century. During this epoch, the two most important changes in the political organization of the Western world were the breakdown of the universality of the Church and the emergence of the Modern State. These developments struck at the heart of the medieval constitutional order by destroying the basis of traditional restraints. By the end of the seventeenth century, it was already clear that the political organization of society had undergone significant alteration. Power was absorbed by emergent new monarchies busily constructing the bureaucratic basis of centralized government. Economic, technological, and social transformations had already eroded the structure of feudalism, but, for a variety of reasons, only the monarchs were efficient and flexible enough to take advantage of those changes. Concomitantly, and in some places as a direct result, Christendom was shattered by the Protestant revolt. With the collapse of the universal Church, the old basis of authority and of sanctions began to break up. External as well as internal restraints upon power gave way to a novel political creation: the nation-state, governed by a new morality—raison d'état.

Modern constitutionalism is a reaction to these developments. It began as an effort to restore some equilibrium to the exercise of power. Its central pillar is still restraint, but restraint built of new materials serving new purposes. Moreover, unlike the organic character of the medieval constitutional order, modern constitutionalism has had to be deliberately planned, fought for, and won, often in violent political and social upheavals. The structure of society no longer favors its automatic continuance. Social power has been enormously expanded and concentrated in the modern world. The preservation of constitutional government, therefore, requires not only the careful construction and deployment of mechanical checks but the persistent and vigorous application of political pressure to ensure that the machinery remains efficient and functional.

The elements of modern constitutional government are these: (1) procedural regularity, (2) substantive limitations, (3) government by consent, (4) spirtual freedom, (5) free expression, and (6) an open political process.

Procedural regularity implies that government can act only by following prescribed patterns of behavior. The formulation and implementation of policy, the enactment and enforcement of laws, and the administration of justice all must be conducted according to established procedural norms. In the Anglo-American tradition, the trenchant phrase "due process of law" has come to be the ultimate standard against which the actual performance of government is measured, particularly in confrontations between the individual and the state.

Substantive limitations go beyond procedural restraints. They are absolute "thou shalt not's" that constitutional government cannot transgress even by following established rules of official conduct. To be sure, such substantive limitations are subject to interpretation and circumvention. In addition, their precise meaning will differ from time to time. In America, for example, the government cannot proscribe freedom of speech, but free speech has a different juridical meaning today than it had two hundred years ago. Nevertheless, despite interpretive variation and historical change, such substantive limitations point to an area of constitutional restraint deserving of even more scrupulous observance than those protected only by procedural defenses.

Modern political thinkers have discovered that the surest guarantee that government will observe prescribed procedures and not exceed its powers is to give to the governed a role in the government itself. The medieval constitution required that taxation, long the most important domestic function of government, be imposed with the consent of those who were to be taxed—a requirement that eventually produced the modern system of representation, whereby the people play an indirect part in the decision-making process through their delegates sitting in representative assemblies. In time, the exercise of the right to vote for delegates—and, later, even for the head of state—became the very signature of constitutional government.

Religious liberty is another vital component of a constitutional order. For centuries, the suppression of religious dissidents was a common occurrence in European public life. Indeed, one of the first demonstrations of muscle by the new national monarchies was the attempt to establish uniformity of belief and worship by compelling allegiance to a single church, threatening execution or exile for those who resisted. To this day, one of the trademarks of some forms of totalitarianism is an atavistic effort to stifle religious institutions and even to destroy religious minorities—part of a relentless drive to root out alternative values and allegiances. Even in otherwise liberal regimes—Britain and the Scandinavian countries, for example—the continuing public support for an official church has caused problems for minority religions as well as for the establishment itself. America was the first to recognize that complete spiritual freedom depended upon the total disengagement of the state from religious affairs.

Freedom of expression is a fifth requisite of constitutionalism. To speak, write, publish, paint, compose, and perform openly and without official constraint has become a defining condition of the free society. The pursuit of social, scientific, and artistic truth must proceed in order for society to produce new knowledge, new ideas, and new ways of looking at, and dealing with, the human condition as it changes. In the field of politics and social thought, in particular, freedom of expression must be maintained if society is to apply to its collective problems the talent, the knowledge, and the wisdom that are so necessary for the discovery and implementation of equitable and viable solutions to social questions.

The vitality of the political process—the sixth essential characteristic of constitutionalism—is necessary in order to keep the avenues to power open and fluid and to prevent a single individual or group from capturing the machinery of force and making it its own. The modern political party system is the chief instrument for achieving this end. Where parties are strong, the other elements of constitutional government will flourish; and where parties are weak, they will be in jeopardy. Indeed, some writers have concluded that the vitality of political parties is the *sine qua non* of modern constitutionalism. Above all, the political process holds government to account.

These, then, are the components of what we call constitutional government: procedural limitations on the way in which government may function; boundaries that define the substance of what government can and cannot do; ways of registering consent and giving to the people a voice in government itself; spiritual and religious liberty; freedom of thought and expression; and a political process that maintains the connections between the government and the people, supplying a mechanism whereby government is made responsive and responsible. Thus, constitutional government is defined by ends and means, by substance and procedure. All are necessary if a constitutional regime can be said to prevail.

Notice, nothing is said here of some favorite American notions of constitutionalism: a written constitution, separate but coequal branches, judicial review, and federalism. These are constitutional practices unique to our system and to those countries that have patterned their governments after ours. And yet, as a people, we have become so accustomed to these special institutions, they have become so central to our concerns, that we often lose sight of what constitutionalism is really all about. But if we allow ourselves to step away from our history and to look at it afresh, we will recognize truths that often escape us. We will see that a relatively high level of constitutionalism was achieved long before the formation of the federal Constitution in 1787. We would realize, too, that, since that Constitution did not, among other things, establish democracy, broaden press freedom, or abolish chattel slavery, it did not automatically usher in a finished constitutional order. To be sure, the Constitution of 1787 served great public purposes. It afforded the heterogeneous American population an elemental rallying point for national unity, and for that reason it was apotheosized very early in our life as an independent republic. But the written Constitution was merely a device for achieving ordered liberty and the prevention of tyranny—it was not thought to be the quintessence of constitutional government, valid for all time.

Jefferson put it best. Though not a member of the Philadelphia Convention, he summarized what must have been the prevailing mood of the Framers in a now famous letter to a friend written in 1816:

> Some men look at constitutions with sanctimonious reverence, and deem them like the ark of the covenant, too sacred to be touched. They ascribe to the men of the preceding age a wisdom more than human, and suppose what they did to be beyond amendment. I knew that age well; I belonged to it, and labored with it. It deserved well of its country. . . . I am certainly not an advocate for frequent and untried changes in laws and constitutions. I think moderate imperfections had better be borne with; because, when once known, we accommodate ourselves to them, and find practical means of correcting their ill effects. But I know also, that laws and institutions must go hand in hand with the progress of the human mind. As that becomes more developed, more enlightened, as new discoveries are made, new truths disclosed, and manners and opinions change with the change of circumstances, institutions must advance also, and keep pace with the times. We might as well require a man to wear still the coat which fitted him when a boy, as civilized society to remain ever under the regimen of their barbarous ancestors.

Our fixation on written constitutional forms—our own in particular—has blinded us to a basic truth: that constitutional government is, at best, a fragile thing beset by novel enemies in every generation. The rhythm of quadrennial Presidential elections, annual sessions of Congress, weekly decisions of courts, and everyday operations of state and local government reassures us that all is well and the Constitution is still in force. Our constitutional history is usually viewed as a chain of court decisions evolving new constitutional doctrine, which forever keeps our fundamental law "abreast of changing times." This fascination with judicial review and what courts have said about the Constitution has so constricted our vision that we often lose sight of the people's responsibility to "keep the watch." The deep but narrow involvement of most of our constitutional historians in the composition, growth, and output of the judiciary has tended to reinforce the central convention of our history: that Revelation occurred at Philadelphia, and all the rest is Commentary. Our constitutional history has been, in a fundamental sense, uncritical. It has abdicated the central responsibility of all written history: to challenge the past, not merely to record it. Afflicted with near-sightedness, we have failed to see that the fight for constitutional government is one that every generation must wage for itself, knowing what it has to lose because it knows what it has already won. As Senator Sam Ervin of North Carolina once put it: "We can never rest on the laurels won by [our] ancestors, nor can we delude ourselves into thinking that our liberties, once having been obtained, are forever secure."

This book is an effort to view our constitutional past in the light of these definitions and standards. Its purpose is to broaden the scope of constitutional history in several ways—first, by examining the colonial past. What is extraordinary about American colonial history is the degree to which a new society, beset by enormous physical problems and located on the edge of a hostile wilderness, succeeded in generating institutions that, in retrospect, represented significant break-throughs and advances in the evolution of Western constitutionalism. In that sense, America was "born modern." The colonial period of our history was, therefore, not only long but exceedingly fruitful. Indeed, it would not require too great a stretch of the historical imagination to say that, in the field of constitutionalism, we have been living on the accumulated capital of colonial ideas and practices. The colonial period comprises about one half of American history if we measure it from 1607, the date of the settlement at Jamestown. For the most part, however, the colonial past has only been ransacked for early precedents of late-eighteenth-century state and federal constitutional models—an effort that diminishes and even distorts the substantial constitutional achievements of colonial Americans in their own right.

This volume asks the kinds of questions of the colonial experience that ought to be applied to the rest of our constitutional history: To what extent were civil liberties recognized? What was the measure of religious liberty? What were the relations between church and state, and what burdens did religious minorities face as a consequence of that relationship? What was the condition of the press? How free or unfree was it? What was the nature of the political process, and how effective was it in keeping the channels to power open? In answering these questions, I have attempted to look at "constitutional reality," not at "constitutional doctrine" or attitudes toward doctrinal questions. Modern studies of the "impact" of court decisions on social behavior should convince us that, when we review the court cases of the past, we only scratch the surface of reality and may still lack even a glimpse of historical truth.

Contrary to a frequent assumption, the structural components of colonial government were probably the least anticipatory of American constitutional arrangements in their mature form. Not long after Independence, the principles that governed relationships between Empire and provinces were abandoned, at both federal and state levels. Moreover, it is difficult to argue that there is a universal structural standard that constitutional governments must follow. We Americans like to believe that we have discovered such a standard in the separation of powers, but the English experience belies this conclusion. Although it is a component of English government, the separation of powers has never been the fundamental and guiding principle of English constitutionalism; yet England has enjoyed constitutional government, in some measure, at least since 1689. Similarly, the institutions of provincial government in America did not function on the basis of the separation-of-powers doctrine, and yet, as I try to show in these pages, substantial progress toward mature constitutionalism was nonetheless achieved.

Yet some attention to structure is important, because the degree to which the formal relationships among discrete organs of government are maintained helps to define the measure of constitutionalism in a particular regime. Moreover, it is necessary to have the structural components of the "colonial constitution" in mind in order fully to understand and appreciate the other elements of colonial constitutionalism. In Chapter 2, I outline this structure emphasizing provincial rather than imperial elements.

Chapter 3 considers the whole question of the extent to which the "rights of Englishmen" were transplanted to America. The problem is three-dimensional. First, did England intend to transplant basic common-law rights? Probably not, since to do so would have undermined the Crown's consistent claim that its power to govern was unrestrained. Second, did the colonists assume that they possessed such rights regardless of English policy and doctrine? From numerous examples of formal colonial enactments claiming English liberties, it is evident that they did. Third, did the colonists implement in practice what these formal enactments recognized in theory? This is the most difficult question to resolve, but, on balance, it appears that the Americans achieved due-process rights equivalent to those enjoyed in England and, in some respects, even surpassed that formidable model.

Chapter 4 describes the relationships between church and state as they changed in the seventeenth and eighteenth centuries. Here, I examine the forces that impelled the rise of religious toleration and would later require the abandonment of state support for religious institutions. The process by which religion was to be liberated from the state—and the state from religion—was not completed before the colonial period ended, but it was far enough advanced for the goal to be visible.

In Chapter 5, I propose a revisionist interpretation of the condition of the press in colonial America. Recent scholarship has established that the laws governing the press were highly restric-

tive, but few have attempted to view this existentially. I suggest
that study of the press in action will show that the impact of the
law has been much exaggerated. Indeed, the colonial press played
a role of increasing importance. Its vigor and contentiousness
both reflected and reinforced the vitality of politics in colonial
public life.

Finally, in Chapter 6, I describe colonial political practices
and then attempt a general assessment of the political process
in the late colonial period. My conclusion, reflective of an increasingly accepted view, is that political controversy was increasingly recognized as a precondition of free government. Politics
was issue-oriented, and political combinations anticipatory of
modern political parties were functioning effectively.

Historians and students of the colonial period will appreciate
how heavily I have leaned on secondary works and well-known
printed sources. I have tried to put some of this material together
in a new way, to view it from a new perspective. In the past
twenty-five years, a great body of writing on the colonial past has
been produced. This book is an effort to synthesize a portion of
it. Each of the chapters is a discrete essay, but together they seek
to establish that, long before the adoption of the written state
and federal constitutions, Americans knew what constitutional
government was about. More importantly, they had established
the basic institutions, practices, and habits of mind of constitutionalism. The colonials did not know that there would be a
Revolution, a break-up of the empire as they had known it, and
a dissolution of the traditional sources of legitimate authority.
They did know that they were a branch of English political and
legal culture, products of England's constitutional struggles of
the seventeenth century, men attached to a regime that was more
liberal than any other then extant in the Western world. At the
very least, they were determined to re-create in America the
foundations for ordered liberty that had been on the agenda of
British politics since 1603. In the end, they achieved even more
than they knew.

2

The Colonial
Constitutional Structure

The governing institutions of the American colonies only partially anticipated the state and federal governments that emerged during and after the Revolution. Like the states, the colonies had governors, legislatures, and courts; they were bound together in an imperial union, just as the states would later enter into a republican federation. But these were surface similarities. At the imperial and provincial level, structural and functional differences were as marked as formal likenesses. The American states would create constitutional organisms with the dry bones of their colonial antecedents, but the product of that effort was, in the end, animated by a desire to reshape the past rather than simply to preserve it.

The clearest demonstration of these differences emerges when we attempt to define the scope of the major organs of provincial authority. One way of approaching such a task would be to look for those political bodies that correspond to the three functions we have associated with modern government: the legislative, the executive, and the judicial. This classical threefold division may have been rendered obsolete by the development of the media as a fourth branch of government and of administrative bureaucracy as a possible fifth, but it still is enshrined in Articles I to III of the Constitution. To search for these bodies, however, is to obscure the issue rather than clarify it. For the fact is that every major provincial institution performed more than one of the functions of government. Governors governed; they did not just "faithfully execute the laws." Legislatures legislated, but they also succeeded in administering much of what their legislation created. And governors and legislatures each acted in a judicial capacity. The court system would emerge only as the legislature recognized its own inability to deal effectively with the rising flood of important litigation—this, plus a determination to prevent the executive from continuing to control the courts. But the courts themselves, even before they became, in some sense, "independent" of the legislatures and the governors, were not confined to judicial affairs. They, too, legislated and administrated. The county courts of the colonial South, for example, were the keystones of local government, performing most public tasks that mattered.

To put it differently, modern American government is based upon the separation of powers—a doctrine of political theory that reached philosophical maturity in the eighteenth century and seemed to rationalize and make sense of the republican structures that Americans were then busily establishing. But the structure of government in the preceding period was not based, even partially, on any such theoretical framework. To colonial Americans, organs of government were not philosophical entities but centers of power, with roots in tradition, staffed by men with competing aims and ambitions, trying to do the public's business in a manner that served the public's good and their own well-being. If anything, those institutions were hegemonic in outlook, with each attempting to do more rather than less. Ideas of functional limitation were of peripheral concern, useful primarily as weapons to defeat the claims of competing bodies. Thus, in examining the structure of colonial government, we must not view it anachronistically through the prism of separation theory but historically, on its own terms, in ways that provincial Americans would have understood.

I

The imperial side of the "colonial constitution" is of great importance in understanding nearly every aspect of colonial public life. For our purposes, however, it is of limited significance. The imperial relation was a special feature of colony governance, just as our federal union is a particular characteristic of American constitutionalism; it is not part of our model of constitutionalism. Still, because of its pivotal role, something needs to be said if what follows is to be clear.

At first, the British colonial empire grew haphazardly; relations between the colonies and the mother country were irregularly coordinated; and the home government lacked effective instruments for achieving central control. Nevertheless, out of the seventeenth-century, Anglo-American imperial experience several recognized and accepted truths did emerge. First, it was undisputed that the colonies were dependencies of England. In constitutional terms, there was no question that ultimate legal authority lay in England; and while some of the colonies managed successfully to evade or undercut the imperial mandate, none questioned its basis. Second, despite the fact that, in the course of the seventeenth century, Parliament reduced the prerogative powers of the monarch—a process completed by the Bloodless Revolution of 1688–89—royal authority to administer, manage, and govern the colonies remained intact. Indeed, with the development of new tools for implementing that control, the sum of royal power in the colonies was actually greater at the end of the seventeenth century than it had been at the beginning. Parliament's capacity, interest, and effectiveness in this area were obviously limited, and, but for intermittent mercantilist enactments—most notably the series of Navigation Acts passed between 1650 and 1696—Parliament was content to leave colonial administration to the King.

There were a number of governmental agencies concerned with the administration of the colonies. The Admiralty inspected cargoes, patrolled the coasts for smugglers and pirates, and protected convoys of merchant ships. Violators of the Navigation Acts were prosecuted in Vice-Admiralty courts. The Treasury saw to the collection of duties and imposts, authorized expenditures, audited colonial accounts, and enforced customs regulations. The large number of officials under its jurisdiction gave the Treasury a considerable presence in the colonies, especially in the proprietary and charter colonies, where royal officials were few in number. The highest official under the King responsible for colonial administration was the Secretary of State for the Southern (European) Department, whose jurisdiction, after 1704, included America. The Secretary of State had a wide variety of administrative and policy-making responsibilities, but undoubtedly his most influential and important role was as the principal dispenser of the colonial patronage.

By 1700, the two most important collective bodies in colonial government were the Privy Council and the recently created Board of Trade. Legally, the Privy Council was the supreme executive agency in the empire. It consisted of the King plus his chief advisers and ministers. It was the Privy Council that issued orders, warrants, and decrees to colonial officials. The Council heard and decided appeals, petitions, and complaints concerning the decisions of provincial courts or the actions taken by provincial legislatures. The Council also established investigatory commissions, issued charters, and formulated instructions for high colonial officials. Before the growth of Cabinet government, the Council was the highest policy-making body in England, and its imprimatur was required for the implementation of most decisions affecting the colonies.

Yet, the great weakness of the Privy Council in the colonial sphere lay in the very breadth of its authority. Concerned with so many affairs of state, it necessarily was incapable of giving more than a fraction of its time and attention to the overseas dominions. As a result, the Council relied upon a subordinate agency commissioned in 1696: the Lords Commissioners of Trade and Plantations, commonly known as the Board of Trade. Consisting of a cadre of experts plus selected members of the Privy Council, the Board became, for a time at least, the primary institution of colonial administration. Though chiefly an advisory group, the Board of Trade developed such expertise in colonial business that its policy guideliness and recommendations for appointment were often followed. As an intelligence-gathering agency constantly preoccupied with provincial disputes and affairs, the Board was a sort of eighteenth-century CIA and at times was regarded by the colonists with about as much suspicion.

In the course of time, the power and influence of the Board of Trade over colonial policy gradually diminished. The Board increasingly deferred to the Secretary of State on appointments. The relentless increase in the costs of colonial administration inevitably pushed the Treasury to the forefront of policy-making. In addition, the Board never achieved real executive power. It remained an advisory group incapable of implementing major policy decisions on its own. Its status remained low in comparison with that of the Treasury and the Admiralty, and for ambitious men it was merely a first step on the ladder to political prominence. Membership on the Board was not sought after by the ablest men in public life as a worthy career goal in itself. The Board did develop a certain competence and experience in colonial affairs, but its own orientation was toward trade and the promotion of the mercantilist program rather than the well-being of the colonies. Thus, the Board of Trade, the one institution of imperial administration primarily concerned with the colonies, was unable to alter what Stanley N. Katz (1968:18) has called the "Anglo-centric, frequently negligent, and generally inconsistent quality of English imperial administration."

Imperial policy was put into effect through these agencies—the Admiralty, the Treasury, the Secretary of State, the Privy Council, and the Board of Trade—by means of administrative devices that circumscribed the decision-making powers of the provincial governments. Officials appointed to colonial offices were given binding instructions as to how they were to perform their duties. The Privy Council retained the right to reverse colonial court decisions and to "disallow" colonial enactments. In time, colonial statutes were required to contain "suspending clauses," which delayed their implementation until the Council had a chance to review them. Finally, the governors themselves were required to veto bills that went against the interest, policies, or laws of England.

It is often said that the imperial relation foreshadowed the American federal system as it emerged under the Constitution of 1787. Support for this view derives from a number of the points briefly sketched in this outline. There was, first of all, a fairly clear distinction between imperial and local concerns. The postal service, trade, naval protection, and over-all foreign and war policy were matters for the imperial authorities, while labor regulation, education, road building, and the like were the sorts of activities that provincial and local authorities were expected to deal with. This fairly clear differentiation of responsibility suggests the kind of "division of powers" that the Constitution later formalized. In addition, there were ways in which the system was coordinated, if not centralized. Privy Council review, after all, did anticipate, even if it did not predetermine, the kind of legal supervision later assumed by the Supreme Court.

On the other hand, a convincing case can be made for the lack of a parallel between England's "federal empire" and the American federal system. The theory of the empire was that the provinces were no more sovereign than English municipalities; but the theory of American federalism is that the states are self-governing and sovereign entities. The whole thrust of English policy in the eighteenth century was toward centralization and subordination, either to the will of Parliament or to that of the Crown. For example, most of the English provinces had been converted into royal colonies by the end of the colonial period, while the semi-autonomous charter colonies—Connecticut, Rhode Island, and Massachusetts—were holdovers from a bygone era, and even Massachusetts had a Crown-appointed governor.

Precisely the reverse was the theory of the American federal union. The evolution of territories into states was to be an evolution *from* dependency *to* autonomy. Indeed, a much better comparison can be drawn between the American territories and the English colonies than between the states and the colonies. U.S. territorial officials would be appointed by the national government to implement policies formulated in the nation's capital. Through the territorial governors, the national administration would participate in local law-making, just as royal appointees played a key role in the decisions of provincial government in the colonial period. But once territories became states, the official connections between state and federal authority broke down. The Constitution would prohibit the President from accepting an "emolument" from any state while in office, and most state constitutions eventually barred federal officials from holding state office or sitting in the state legislatures. Both governments—the state and the federal—were sovereign, and this *dual sovereignty* supplanted the simple hierarchical arrangements, based upon the single sovereign, that were the cornerstone of the Empire.

What brought about the crisis of Independence, in the middle of the eighteenth century, was precisely the failure of the English Government to recognize its political inability to compel the provinces to conform to the theory and practice of unitary sovereignty, colonial dependency, and centralized control. Colonial rejection of the imperial relation led to the creation of the very differently conceived American federal union of independent and sovereign states.

II

The key figure in the public life of the colonies was the governor, a royal or proprietary appointee in all but two of the provinces by the end of the colonial period. A vice-regent for the King in most places, the governor enjoyed legal powers that, curiously, surpassed those exercised in eighteenth-century England by the monarch himself. Indeed the governor continued Stuarts rather than what it had become in the age of the Hanoverians. His legal powers were considerable. As set forth in a typical mid-eighteenth-century commission—the instrument that conveyed to the governor his office and, in the royal provinces at least, was the functional equivalent to a written constitution— these powers encompassed broad parameters of authority:

- —to execute the laws and all things under his command and trust
- —to call together assemblies of the freeholders or their deputies
- —with the assent of the legislature, "to make, constitute and ordain Laws, Statutes and Ordinances for the publick Peace, Welfare and good Government" of the province
- —to exercise an absolute veto over laws, statutes, and ordinances passed in the legislature but contrary to the interest or policy of the Crown
- —to adjourn, prorogue, or dissolve assemblies when he deemed it necessary
- —"to erect, constitute and appoint such and so many Courts of Judicature and publick justice" for hearing "all causes, as well Criminal as Civil, according to Law and Equity"

—to appoint judges, justices of the peace, and commissioners of *oyer* and *terminer** "for the better Administration of Justice"

—to grant pardons for most criminal offenses and temporary reprieves to traitors and willful murderers

—to command military and naval forces to repel attack from land or sea, to appoint military officers, and, when necessary, to execute martial law

—to issue warrants for the expenditure of public monies

—to create fairs, markets, ports, and harbors

—to collate ministers of the Church to ecclesiastical benefices †

Such substantial authority granted to the royal governor in America enabled him to fulfill multiple responsibilities: to carry out the secret instructions that periodically informed him of changes in imperial policy; to execute relevant parliamentary statutes—the Navigation Acts, in particular; and to execute the laws of his province. Not surprisingly, these responsibilities frequently conflicted, and governors were often caught in crosscurrents of competing forces. Instructions could modify and even erode powers granted in commission. Local pressures and interests might cause the governor to hedge his strict adherence to policy formulated by the King in Council or even to contravene his bonded oath to enforce parliamentary enactments. If the conflict was sharp and well-defined, then the governor knew his priorities and would support general imperial interests over local provincial demands; but usually his course of action was not clear, and he applied his discretion at great personal and political risk.

What is most important to notice, however, is the relative clarity of the governor's office when it is looked upon as an instrument of power and its ambiguity when defined in terms of function. That is to say, the governorship was an office with sufficient legal authority to carry out tasks that went beyond executive duties. Thus, the governor was expected to see that law was enforced, but he was also authorized to create much of it. In the seventeenth century, the initiative for legislation came

---

* Commissions of *oyer* and *terminer* empowered judges to try cases involving treason, felony, and/or misdemeanor.

† Based upon the Commission to Francis Bernard, Governor of New Jersey, 1758.

from the governor; he outlined measures for legislative enactment in great detail and did not merely transmit the broad policy directives of the Lords of Trade. In effect, the governor proposed the laws and the legislature gave or withheld its assent—precisely the reverse of the pattern that became standard in the eighteenth century, when it was the legislature that claimed the responsibility to initiate legislation, reserving to the governor the right to assent or apply his absolute veto. Moreover, executive ordinances and proclamations, not requiring the legislature's approval, had the force of enacted law. In 1699, for example, New York's Governor Bellomont renewed the Judiciary Act of 1691 by executive proclamation when the assembly failed to do so by statute. New York's Supreme Court was continued for the rest of the colonial era by executive ordinance. Executive ordinances also established a chancery court in New York, despite assembly objections to what it perceived as a usurpation of the legislature's business. Similar examples of governors' creating or continuing courts can be found for other colonies. Except in Rhode Island and Connecticut, where written charters established the legislature's right to erect courts of law, the issue was bitterly contested. The Crown, acting through the governors, insisted to the end that the creation of courts of law and courts of equity was a prerogative power, and not within the jurisdiction of the provincial legislatures.

Not only did the appointed governors claim to have lawmaking competence, which their continuing efforts to establish courts of justice without legislative sanction illustrates, but they frequently served in a judicial capacity. In the absence of regular church courts, which in England dealt with probate, marriage, and divorce, the governors probated wills and issued divorce decrees or delegated their authority to do so to others, reserving the right to hear petitions on appeal. Of even more consequence were the chancery powers that provincial governors possessed as custodians of the province seal. In New York, New Jersey, Maryland, and South Carolina—the only colonies where separate chancery courts existed for a considerable period of time—the governor served as the court of equity, sometimes with and sometimes without his council. Governors also enjoyed the power to sit as high appellate courts. Governors and councils were the final courts of appeal in civil cases above a minimum property value and in some criminal cases. Review in the proprietary colonies was lodged in the superior courts; in the charter colonies of Rhode Island and Connecticut, it was lodged in the assembly; but in most of the royal provinces, the governor exercised appellate review, a legacy of the time when governors sitting in council held regular trials and dispensed justice as a routine function of office. In Virginia, right to the end of the colonial era, the governor (or his deputy) and the council served as the highest provincial trial court—the General Court—exercising broad jurisdiction in criminal and civil disputes. Thus, the colonial governors did not confine their official activities to those we associate with the "chief executive"; they also legislated and adjudicated. Government was a unitary thing, and governors acted in accordance with that fundamental conception.

III

Functional ambiguity was just as evident, perhaps even more so, in the governor's council—an institutional cross between an upper legislative chamber, a cabinet, and a privy council, whose actual power gradually diminished as a result of its fundamental political weakness and its failure to develop any independent initiative or authority. Except in Massachusetts, where the council was elected by the legislature and approved by the governor, councilmen were appointees of the Crown. Their chief purpose was to serve, as their title implied, as advisers to the governor in such important areas of decision as appointments, expenditures, the calling of the assembly, legislation, Indian policy, and the like. In most of these matters, the governor's commission usually required conciliar consultation, but only at the solicitation of the governor. Thus, the council was first and foremost an executive body and could be likened to a royal council of key advisers. As we have seen, in many colonies the governor in council served as a court of appeal somewhat similar to the English Privy Council, which, by virtue of its administrative control over colonial litigation and legislation, acted as an agency of judicial review. The Privy Council, however, had long since ceased to be a final court of appeal in the realm itself. Consequently, by the end of the seventeenth century, the King in Council was no longer part of the judicial structure, but in most of the colonies the governor in council still was—another instance of the peculiar anachronism of colonial legal and governmental institutions that, for various reasons, resembled earlier rather than contemporary English models.

The likeness between the colonial councils and the Privy Council, however, had serious limitations. What most strikingly distinguished the colonial council from its executive counterpart in England was that, in the provinces, it served as the upper chamber of the provincial legislature, except in Pennsylvania, where the legislature was unicameral. The upper chamber's concurrence in all legislation was mandatory, but it was precisely here that the council ran into greatest difficulty. The council was usually the handmaiden of the governor. Its members owed their position, and perhaps other high provincial offices as well, to his favor. As a result of conciliar ability to act independently in legislative concerns was permanently compromised. A council sat legislatively in a double capacity: first as an upper chamber; then as a collective adviser to the governor, whose assent was required to make bills into laws. And there are instances of councils' having approved proposals as upper chambers and subsequently advising the governor to reject the same proposals. Councilmen were easily intimidated by a strong governor, and the presence of such a governor in their deliberations was a source of institutional weakness. In 1725, the law officers of the Crown ruled that governors could no longer sit with the council when it was considering and voting on legislation, but the ruling was not immediately complied with in all cases; in New York, the governor did not withdraw until 1730; in New Jersey, not until 1738; and in South Carolina, not until 1756.

The withdrawal of the governors from the council sitting as an upper house should have contributed to its maturation as an independent body, but too many other weaknesses stood in the way. In most colonies, the total number of councilors was small, usually twelve. Quorums were even smaller. In 1744, Governor

James Glen of South Carolina reported that the business of the upper chamber was occasionally conducted with no more than three, two, and even one councilman present—hardly an indication of institutional viability. Too small to organize the kind of regular committee system that would enable the lower houses of assembly to achieve real legislative competence, the upper houses remained subservient to either a strong executive or a strong lower house. Often, they were caught between the two. Failing to develop any kind of independent initiative, usually unable to proffer unsolicited advice to the governor, and not representing a distinct political constituency, the colonial councils became a casualty of the Revolution. Their demise was brought on by multiple forces, not the least of which was the very ambiguity of their function. Authorized to do much, they wound up able to do little.

IV

The most consequential component of provincial government, besides the governor himself, were the lower houses of assembly. These were the institutions that would lead the provinces in the crisis of Independence, would write the first state constitutions, and, at least for a time, would replace the executives in public leadership as the American states emerged from the incubus of British colonialism. Their steady, sometimes rapid, growth in initiative, competence, and power in the century preceding the Revolution is dramatic. Indeed, it was the effort to reassert the royal *prerogative*, reinforced by parliamentary enactments, at the expense of assembly *privilege* that brought on the imperial crisis of the 1760's.

There is some debate about the relative power of the lower houses of assembly vis-à-vis the colonial governors. The most substantial work to date has argued persuasively that the general tendency was toward the aggrandizement of power by the assembly and the consequent erosion of executive prerogative. In a detailed examination of the assemblies in the four royal colonies of the South—Virginia, the Carolinas, and Georgia—Jack P. Greene (1963) has seen a steady, though unplanned, displacement of traditional gubernatorial prerogatives. This "rise of the assembly" can be found, Greene suggests, throughout the colonies. It was the most significant constitutional development of the late colonial period. J. R. Pole (1966), a student of representative institutions in colonial and early America, is in accord with this view.

On the other hand, several critics of the "assembly power" thesis have pointed to the considerable authority retained by colonial executives. John M. Murrin (1965) refers to the "myth of royal decline" in the eighteenth century and argues that, in the area of colonial administration, the Crown sought efficient government at the expense of traditional assembly privilege. In the colonies, royal authority exercised through the colonial governors was on the increase. Robert Zemsky (1971) is sympathetic to this view and illustrates the argument by pointing to the wide range of powers held by the chief executive in Massachusetts. Still a third position attempts to reconcile these opposite theses. Stanley N. Katz (1968) writes that "to speak of 'the rise of the assembly' as the determining factor in colonial politics in this period is to distort its importance." Katz argues that governors and assemblies in New York managed to work out their differences in mutually beneficial compromise arrangements that were rooted in economic and familial rather than in institutional or ideological needs. Bernard Bailyn (1968) asserts that, while the formal constitutional powers of the governors in the royal (and even in the proprietary) colonies remained intact, their real leverage had been seriously undermined by certain inherent weaknesses in their political position. The governors enjoyed "swollen claims and shrunken powers"—a phrase that aptly summarizes this middle view.

Whatever the direction or tendency of the assemblies' constitutional power relative to that of the colonial executives, however, their activity was marked by the same kind of crossing over of functional lines that we saw as characteristic of the other main bodies of provincial government. Unlike the council, which initially enjoyed wide-ranging authority by virtue of its close attachment to the governor, the assemblies started with a narrow mandate. The first colonial governors recognized that assemblies

of freeholders or their deputies were necessary if the colony was
to flourish, but the initial purpose of these early gatherings was
to vote supplies and to sanction measures proposed above. The
theory was that the executive made the laws and the people,
through their assemblies, consented to them. Assemblies were
called in to play an integral and necessary, but clearly subordinate, part in government and administration.

Their functions were few. As Governor Richard Nicolls put
it in an address to the inhabitants of Long Island soon after the
English displaced the Dutch in New York:

> In discharge . . . of my Trust and Duty, to Settle good and
> knowne Laws within this government for the future, and receive
> your best advice and Information in a General Meeting, I have
> thought fitt to Publish unto you, That upon the last day of this
> present February, at *Hempsteed* upon *Long Island,* shall be held
> a Generall Meeting which is to consist of Deputyes chosen by the
> major part of the freemen only.

Most seventeenth-century calls for assemblies of freeholders were
more expansive and less peremptory than this one, but the language summoning the inhabitants of Long Island to send delegates to New York's first brief experiment with representative
government captures the spirit of the time. As the Duke of York,
in more moderate tones, instructed Governor Thomas Dongan
in 1683:

> . . . there shall be a Generall Assembly of all the Freeholders . . .
> to [consult] with yourselfe and the . . . Council what laws are fitt
> and necessary to be made and established for the good weale and
> government of the said Colony and its Dependencyes, and of all
> the inhabitants thereof.

By the end of the seventeenth century, the initial subordination of the assemblies to the other organs of provincial government had ended. The lower houses had won the right to meet
separately, to elect their own speaker, to maintain standing committees and appoint special ones, to shield their members from
arrest, to decide disputed elections, and to protect members' rights

to speak freely in debate. The colonial assemblies claimed to be little parliaments. Nourished by books and manuals outlining legislative procedure in England, the assemblies modeled themselves after the House of Commons, although neither Parliament nor legal doctrine supported such a parallel.

But from the very beginning, the assemblies expanded their responsibilities beyond the specific mandate that had brought them into being. They moved into areas of activity far beyond what we would consider the normal duties of a legislature, and, as the colonial period progressed, the exercise of these multiple responsibilities became even more decided. For example, assemblies exercised judicial power. There are numerous instances of this from the records of early Virginia and Maryland. Judicial disputes resolved in the legislature in this period involved such matters as insubordination of servants, treasonous utterances, avoidance of impost charges, rebellion, slander, piracy, murder, and assault. Punishments meted out were the same as those common to courts in the seventeenth century—fine, pillory, whipping, and imprisonment. Even the word "sentence" was used. During the first decades of their existence, the assemblies consisted of the governor, the council, and the freemen or their delegates sitting together. Later on, the deputies achieved the right to sit separately—the prerequisite for the development of the lower house as an independent body. Judicial proceedings thereafter often took on the character of an impeachment, with the lower house preferring charges for decision by the upper chamber. Nevertheless, there were a few cases in Maryland, in the early eighteenth century, where the lower house alone tried minor cases, imposed penalties, and even asserted that it was the "highest court of judicature" in the province, an assertion that the upper house naturally resented.

From early New England comes similar evidence of legislatures acting as courts, with the lower houses claiming equivalent judicial authority to that of the upper chamber, the "Court of Assistants." In fact, the separation of the House of Deputies from the Assistants—the starting point for bicameralism in Massachusetts—came about as a result of an appeal, in 1642, to the General Court (that is, the provincial legislature) of a lower-court decision concerning the disputed ownership of a wayward pig. The famous case of the stray sow, *Sherman* v. *Keayne,* was decided in favor of the defendant, even though a majority of the legislature voted for the plaintiff; this, because the collective voice of the Assistants (who favored Keayne) superseded that of the Deputies (who favored Sherman). The Deputies objected to the exercise of a virtual veto power by the Assistants, and soon thereafter determined that the two bodies should meet separately, with the concurrence of both required for the enactment of bills into law. Moreover, judicial appeals were to be heard by the entire legislature sitting as a single group and deciding by a simple majority vote.

In the colony of Plymouth, the General Court received grand-jury presentments, heard coroner jury reports, conducted trials, and handed down punishments. As a leading historian of the colonial legislatures once concluded, "It is doubtful if any other representative assembly in the colonies ever conducted so many criminal prosecutions or inflicted so many punishments in a like period of time as did that of Plymouth" (Clarke, *Parliamentary Privilege,* 1943:25). Elsewhere, assemblies heard and granted petitions for divorce, supervised lower-court proceedings, and "moved" law-enforcement officials to do justice when they were lax in their duties. In some colonies, the power to pardon was lodged in the legislatures. Petitions for relief of various kinds were usually placed before the lower house, which often responded on its own without consulting the upper chamber. Court judgments could be vacated or overturned either by legislative enactment or by independent action on the part of the assembly.

In general, it is clear that colonial legislatures exercised significant judicial authority. With the growth of bicameralism, judicial business gravitated toward the upper chambers, but the lower houses continued to play an important judicial role. Even as the courts assumed the major burden of litigation, legislatures retained the power to supervise judicial activity. Their reluctance to surrender high judicial authority is evidenced, in most of the colonies, by the very slow attainment by high courts of justice of the right to issue writs of mandamus—the prerogative writ whose possession by the courts would have signified their full maturation and their independence from the legislative and executive bodies that had created them. The wooden "bar" of the lower house, usually put in place at its very first session, was the symbol of that body's judicial authority, as many who were called to kneel before it could fully testify.

Although they preserved important residual competence to act as courts—the power to impeach and to grant relief to private petitioners representing but two examples—the judicial power of the lower houses of assembly was eventually eclipsed by the development of the court system. But if the activities of the assemblies functioning as courts of law was in relative decline in the eighteenth century, legislative claims to executive power were on the increase. When historians speak of the "rise of the assembly" in this period, they are referring to this feature of their institutional growth.

What was taking place in America was a duplication of parliamentary history, except that it was happening within a much more concentrated time-frame. Until the sixteenth century, Parliament was a subordinate branch of English government. The infrequency and short duration of its meetings in the Tudor period are the best evidence of its weakness. By the time of the early Stuarts, however, the Commons had achieved royal recognition of some elementary "privileges of the house": to decide disputed elections; to discipline and, if necessary, expel objectionable members; to shield deputies from "molestation" or arrest; and to protect their freedom of speech in debate. Not that these "privileges" were secure from royal interference, but they did establish the basis for the assertion by Parliament—the House of Commons, in particular—of its right to function as a regular, independent, and coordinate part of the English constitution.

The precondition for the Stuart Restoration in 1660 was the implicit acknowledgment by Charles II of Parliament's right to exist. No longer could the King govern constitutionally without Parliament. Only by virtue of its participation with Parliament in law-making would the Crown continue to enjoy pre-eminence in the realm. When William and Mary were invited to the throne, following the Revolution of 1688, the basis was estab-

lished for the emergence in the eighteenth century of the "supremacy" of Parliament in English government—a theory that
achieved systematic formulation in Sir William Blackstone's
Commentaries on the Laws of England (1765–69), published on
the very eve of the American Revolution.

It was this history that the colonial assemblies were both con-
sciously and inadvertently re-enacting in America. Starting out
as subordinate agents called in to assist the governors and proprietors of the early settlements, the assemblies would achieve,
in the course of a century, a status of equality in the colonial
constitutional framework. By the middle of the eighteenth century, their movement toward supremacy—not unlike that of Parliament in England—was becoming a marked feature of the
provincial scene. As James Glen, royal governor of South Carolina, remarked in 1748, "the People," through the assembly,
"have got the whole administration into their Hands, and the
Crown is by various Laws despoiled of its principal flowers and
brightest Jewels."

But it was the assertion of what we would call executive
authority that the "quest for power" on the part of the colonial
assemblies was most noticeable. This was attempted in a number
of key areas. In control of the taxing power by virtue of traditional English custom and local usage, the provincial assemblies
asserted their absolute control over all money bills and their
right to oversee the expenditure of the funds they voted to raise.
At first, they insisted on auditing executive accounts. Later, they
began to make detailed appropriations for specific undertakings
and to appoint the men charged with the responsibility for
carrying them out. Some assemblies extended their traditional
control of executive income, especially the governor's, by setting
fee rates, normally an executive function. Perhaps most significant of all was the effort to take control of Indian affairs and
intercolonial relations—two areas of "foreign policy" that the
Crown permitted the governors to handle in its name, but which
the assemblies seemed bent on usurping. Assemblies tried to gain
control over the appointment of key provincial officials customarily in the gift of the governor: the public printer, the colonial
agent, military officers, paymasters, revenue collectors, the colony

treasurer, and the comptroller. In addition, some assemblies, through the appointment of special commissioners, took on routine administrative tasks: supervising the construction of forts, bridges, lighthouses, churches, canals, and other public works; and seeing to the improvement of navigation, port facilities, poor relief, education, and market operations—tasks that normally fell either to the governor or to local agencies of government.

To effectuate their claim to executive competence, the lower houses tried to overcome certain structural weaknesses in their composition. Unlike the councils, which were continuous bodies, the assemblies met irregularly and depended upon the governor to call them and keep them in session, except where, as in Massachusetts, Connecticut, and Rhode Island, meetings at specified intervals were mandated by charter. To overcome this serious handicap, the assemblies attempted to duplicate Parliament's history by passing biennial or triennial acts (laws requiring the calling of the assembly into session at least every two or three years) and septennial acts (which required an election of a new assembly at least once in seven years). Only a few of the royal colonies, however, managed to enact such legislation. New York passed a septennial law in 1743, and New Hampshire and South Carolina each had triennial acts. Assemblies also established committees, some of which dealt with the legislature's own business—the standing committee on privileges and elections, for example—but others, such as the standing committees on trade, courts of justice, and religion as well as extraordinary committees set up from time to time, dealt with general policy that traditionally had been the concern of the executive. The formation of the committee system is illustrative of the desire on the part of the legislature to duplicate executive functions in the administration of provincial government. The establishment of special extrasessionary committees to meet when the assemblies were not in session evidenced the desire to maintain constitutional continuity equivalent to that of the council and even of the governor himself.

There was, of course, no perfect uniformity in the "encroachment" of the legislature upon the domain of the executive from colony to colony. What is particularly interesting, however, is that the provincial lower houses, especially in the eighteenth century, were more successful in sharing a wide range of executive responsibilities than in establishing, once and for all, undisputed control over key legislative privileges. The failure of most colonial assemblies to secure the right to control the frequency of elections, the length of legislative sessions, or the apportionment of seats in the house at the same time that they succeeded in carving out large chunks of executive authority even surpassing those enjoyed by the House of Commons is one of the anomalies of colonial constitutional history.

V

Colonial courts, particularly at the local level, manifested a similar tendency to exercise power rather than simply to adjudicate disputes. Southern county courts provide the best illustration of this. In Virginia, the Carolinas, Georgia, and Maryland, where towns and cities were very few and population less concentrated than in the Middle Colonies and New England, the county was the pivot of government. The county court, consisting of eight to thirty judges appointed by the governor, usually for an indefinite term, represented the entrenched local oligarchy and controlled the levers of effective power and administration. Even at the provincial level, power flowed from the counties upward rather than from the center outward. The colonial assemblies were made up of delegates from the counties, elected by county and representing the men of wealth, standing, and influence in the counties, just as in New England the provincial assemblies represented the towns and the structure of power located in the towns rather than the people at large.

County courts were first and foremost courts of justice that dealt with civil disputes above a minimum amount and with serious criminal offenses the punishment for which would be less than loss of life, limb, or estate. But these courts did much more. They had important economic, social, political, and administrative functions equal to, if not actually greater than, their judicial role. County courts set the terms for the acquisition and transfer of land titles; they supervised the drafting of labor contracts for indentured workers; and they regulated the treatment of servants and slaves. The county court was responsible for the construction and maintenance of roads, bridges, streets, and wharves and for the upkeep of navigation on rivers and streams. For these purposes, the county nominated commissioners and surveyors, who, though appointed by the governor, had to answer to the court, which was charged by provincial statute with responsibility for seeing to these matters. In addition, the county courts regulated the practice of professions and trades by issuing licenses and setting fee schedules and price lists.

Acting through the sheriffs and commissioners of revenue, the county courts collected both local and general taxes. They supervised the marketing of staple commodities, kept standard weights and measures, and established procedures for grading and inspecting goods sold for export. The county court served as a local conservation authority, ordering the destruction of pests and the observance of game regulations. On the social side, the court was responsible for poor relief and the upholding of public morals and true religion, although most of these responsibilities were parceled out to the parishes—the major subdivisions of the county in the colonial South. The county also took care of orphans and saw to their education and apprenticeship. In time of war, the county had to levy troops for the militia; it supplied them with provisions, ammunition, and housing, occasionally even having to finance and build fortifications for their defense.

In short, the county courts discharged the major public functions affecting everyday life. They did so by exercising their capacity to pass bylaws and ordinances and, through their judicial authority, to enforce their observance. In combining these separate functions of government, the county court of the colonial era seems to have anticipated the modern administrative agency, but, in point of fact, it was more a traditional institution than a prematurely modern one. It was, perhaps, the archetypical public body exercising power as a whole rather than in neatly compartmentalized and divided functions.

Only in the higher courts was this tendency muted. Indeed, it is in the emergence of the judicial role as separate and distinct from the executive that the functional differentiation of governmental power achieved theoretical clarity. The judiciary in America was not independent in any real sense during the colonial period. The legislature—the lower house, in particular—had deep roots in English tradition and weighty political support in the province. The governor also had substantial political resources. In most cases, his appointment was a product of his political connections in England. Moreover, his legal position as the representative of the Crown was a source of great power. But the courts shared none of these elements of independent support. In England, the courts had achieved real institutional security: They were the custodians of the common law, which only Parliament could alter; the King had lost his power to create courts of justice; and the Act of Settlement (1701) made judges subject to removal only "upon address" by both Houses of Parliament, thus removing the judiciary from the normal pressures of executive influence.

But in America, the reception of the English common law was problematical, and courts could hardly claim more independence than the law they adjudicated was acknowledged to possess. Moreover, in America the courts continued to be creatures of either the executives or the legislatures that had created and conceivably could terminate them at will. Finally, the Crown never recognized tenure during good behavior for colonial judges. They usually served "during the King's pleasure"—that is, until either the King or the governor in council decided to replace them for exigent causes.

There are some isolated instances of judges enjoying good-behavior tenure. Governor Lewis Morris appointed his son Robert Hunter Morris to the Chief Justiceship of New Jersey in 1739 with a good-behavior commission. In New York, the Chief Justice of the Supreme Court, James De Lancey, as well as the associate judges, served during good behavior. De Lancey's death, in 1760, brought a confrontation between the assembly, which favored continuing the De Lancey precedent, and Lieutenant Governor Cadwallader Colden, who wanted New York to conform to the regular custom. Eventually, the issue was temporarily resolved when, in November, 1761, the King in Council issued new instructions ordering all governors not to submit to legislative attempts to establish good-behavior tenure, and Colden succeeded in getting judges to serve during pleasure.

The cry for "an independent judiciary" was more an effort on the part of the assemblies to deprive the agents of the royal prerogative of an important political tool than a selfless demand for good government. The clamor continued throughout the colonies, and the failure of the Crown to compromise on this issue added another argument to the mounting opposition to prerogative power in America.

Buffeted between these contending forces, with the Crown on one side and the assemblies on the other, the courts lacked the independence that their English counterparts enjoyed. Yet, despite inherent weaknesses, the judicial system in most of the colonies was so articulated during the eighteenth century that the courts had become indispensable. This was their major source of strength.

The judicial structure, like so many other features of colonial life, was not uniform from one province to another, but a number of salient characteristics were shared by all. First, colonial court systems did not attempt to duplicate the wide variety of courts that still existed in England as a legacy of centuries of accumulation. The colonial judicial system was more unified and integrated, and local law administered by separate and distinct local courts did not take root in America. Second, the colonies, with some exceptions, rejected the bifurcation between law courts and equity courts that was the distinguishing mark of England's national judicial system. Americans wanted equity law but not equity courts, and in most of the colonies regular law courts or legislative assemblies applied equitable remedies to achieve substantial justice. Third, the court systems in America were more clearly hierarchical than those in England. Inferior courts were set up to deal with minor offenses and petty disputes and "superior" or "supreme" courts for serious crimes and civil causes of a minimum value. Gradually, the higher courts gained supervisory control over the lower courts through such devices as the power to issue writs of mandamus. Fourth, because of unevenness in technical competence—usually only the chief judge of the province had legal training, while his associates were laymen—

the right of appeal was widely accepted in America. Thus, "courts of appeal"—normally the governor and his council—exercised the power to review errors in the record of the trial court below. Finally, while it was devised as a method of securing administrative control of colonial affairs, the review of American court decisions by the Privy Council established at least the precedent for a single agency or court of review to apply uniform standards of law and procedure to the colonies as a whole. While the number of cases appealed to the Privy Council was relatively small and the Council did not develop a body of precedents or a means of reporting its decisions, the very existence of Privy Council review served as a check upon colonial courts and forced litigants to predict what the Council would determine should an appeal go that far.

VI

The agitation for, and the emergence of, the judiciary as an independent agency—a development still in process at the end of the colonial period—ignited interest in the evolving doctrine of the separation of powers. That theory of political architecture had a long history by the mid-eighteenth century. As a result of the English Civil War and the constitutional debates it had engendered, separation of powers had come to mean merely the separation of the executive and legislative functions. Constitutional government required that those making the laws and those executing them be separate and distinct. As John Locke put it in his *Second Treatise on Government* (chap. 12):

> . . . because it may be too great a temptation to human frailty, apt to grasp at power, for the same persons who have the power of making laws, to have also in their hands the power to execute them. . . . therefore in well ordered commonwealths . . . the legislative power is put into the hands of diverse persons, who duly assembled, have by themselves, or jointly with others, a power to make them. . . . But because the laws, that are at once, and in a short time made, have a constant and lasting force, and need a perpetual execution, or an attendance thereunto; therefore it is necessary there should be a power always in being, which should

see to the execution of the laws that are made, and remain in force. And thus the legislative and executive power come often to be separated.

Locke conceived of what he called a "federative power"—in effect, power to conduct foreign policy—but he considered it part of the executive and not to be separated from it.

Baron de Montesquieu, the great eighteenth-century student of government, was not the first to conceive of the more familiar tripartite division, but he did give it greater publicity and a more empirical cast than had any previous writer:

> . . . there is no liberty, if the judiciary power be not separated from the legislative and executive. Were it joined with the legislative, the life and liberty of the subject would be exposed to arbitrary control; for the judge would be then the legislator. Were it joined to the executive power, the judge might behave with violence and oppression. There would be an end of everything, were the same body, whether of the nobles or of the people, to exercise those three powers, that of enacting laws, that of executing the public resolutions, and of trying the causes of individuals [*The Spirit of the Laws,* Book XI].

Here, the judicial function emerges as a separate, though not necessarily a coequal, branch of government, and this at a time when judicial independence was a hotly contested issue in most of the American colonies.

For a number of reasons, the separation-of-powers doctrine did not become dominant in England as it did in America. After the Revolution of 1688–89, it was overshadowed by the "balanced constitution" and "mixed government" notions that were in some ways opposite to the separation theory. Moreover, the "place acts" passed by Parliament in this period had the effect of diminishing one of the principal reasons why separation of powers was to continue to have greater appeal in America. The English statutes, principally the Succession to the Crown Act of 1707 and the Place Act of 1742, provided that revenue collectors, commissioners, low civil servants and secretaries, paymasters, pensioners, and other Crown appointees be either excluded from sitting in the House of Commons or forced to stand for election after their appointment. This by no means ended the problem of the "place-men" in Parliament—important officials appointed by the King's ministers rather than by the Crown directly were not covered by the statutes, and the requirement that "placemen" stand for election was not significant because most of them were returned by their constituents—but it did blunt some of the radical criticism that viewed plural officeholding as a corruption of the constitutional settlement.

In America, however, although some colonies passed "place acts," the problem of plural officeholding remained an acute cause of complaint. In Massachusetts, members of the governor's council often held high judicial or administrative posts. Most of the judges of the Superior Court sat on the council at one time or another. Thomas Hutchinson's career typified the excesses of the practice. Hutchinson was Lieutenant Governor, a councilman, the probate judge for Suffolk County, and the military commander on Castle Island when he was appointed Chief Justice of Massachusetts in 1762. Members of the Massachusetts council usually held at least one judicial position, a fact that caused simple practical problems—they could not be in two places at once. Court responsibilities often prevented them from attending to council business. Indeed, in Massachusetts the agitation for the independence of the judiciary was directly related to the inefficiency of having judges occupy more than one place at a time. Separation of powers was formally adopted, in principle, by the state of Massachusetts in its constitution of 1780, but as Ellen E. Brennan (1945:vii) concluded, "The custom of plural officeholding [was] one of the chief factors which led to the adoption of provisions for a separation of departments of government in the Massachusetts Constitution."

Elsewhere, the controversy may not have been quite so sharp as in Massachusetts, but plural officeholding remained a ubiquitous problem. Although the colonial governors lacked the sizable patronage available to the King, and although assembly encroachment continued to erode the executive power of appointment, fear of placemen and the ongoing practice of plural officeholding had much to do with increasing the interest in separation of powers when state legislatures and conventions began drafting new frames of government after Independence was declared.

Separation of powers was not, however, one of the first fruits of the American Revolution. As Gordon S. Wood (1969:chap. 4) has pointed out, while most of the new state constitutions established in the initial flush of revolutionary zeal adhered to it in principle, in practice their departures from the doctrine in its purer forms were pronounced. In fact, while the times were redolent with the sense of newness, and while legislators and constitution-makers were thrilled by the opportunity for social and political experimentation, the initial efforts to restructure the framework of colony government drew upon and fulfilled the tendencies of the past more than they pointed the way to the future. Not until the period of what might be called the constitutional backlash of the 1780's and 1790's were these first, radical state structures modified and the modern pattern of American government revealed, the federal Constitution of 1787 itself being the outstanding product of that conservative reaction.

By the mid-eighteenth century, separation of powers meant that the functions of government were to be kept apart by separating the agencies, or departments, that performed those functions and by barring the personnel of one from serving simultaneously in another. This form of the doctrine, however, was used selectively in the early years of Independence, mostly as a way of justifying the enhancement of the legislatures at the expense of the governors. Legislative power to appoint and to impeach; to appropriate, spend, and supervise expenditures; to declare war and to conduct foreign policy—these and other traditionally executive prerogatives were taken over by many of the new state legislatures in the first months of Independence. Executive officers were barred from sitting in the legislature. Courts of chancery and courts of appeal were substituted for the old governors and their councils. Judges were elected by the people and were removable by legislative "address," and their tenure of office was limited to a fixed number of years. Upper houses of the legislature were established, with members barred from serving as either judges or councilors. All these changes had the effect of defining responsibilities more precisely and eliminating the functional ambiguities of the colonial regime, but the thrust behind them was not scrupulous adherence to a new theory of government but the old drive to power by the most dynamic branch of colonial government, the legislative assemblies. The General Court of Massachusetts, as established under the Constitution of 1780, for example, continued to act as a court and to give detailed attention to the supervision of the state judicial system. In executive affairs, it relegated the governor of the state to a clearly subordinate position, directing him to carry out military plans adopted by the legislature and to answer to the legislature for their execution.

In effect, the early state constitutions codified the "encroachments" of the colonial period, transferred the primary dependence of the courts from the executive to the legislature and the people, and reduced the governor's office to that of an administrator. One state, Pennsylvania, abandoned the office of governor altogether by substituting a council of twelve for the single executive. The colonial experience had pointed toward a system of legislative supremacy. Certainly the parliamentary model, which the colonial assemblies had emulated and even exceeded when they could, was attractive. But for reasons that went beyond merely structural concerns, legislative supremacy was ultimately rejected and a rather conservative version of separation of powers, mixed with an elaborate system of checks and balances among roughly equal branches, was put in its place. Hence, the structure of the colonial constitution did not survive the Revolution intact. It was important in helping to shape the ideas and institutions that grew out of it, but contributed to the development of the enduring forms of American government by serving more as a model that was largely abandoned than as one that was substantially preserved.

3

The Legal Rights of Early Americans

I

For many years, legal historians have been measuring the degree to which early American law either diverged from or duplicated English law. The pioneer scholars in this field, deeply influenced by Frederick Jackson Turner's themes of frontier nationalism and American uniqueness, emphasized the wide disparities between English and American law in the colonial period, but more recent writers have tended to point to the parallels and similarities between American law and English common law or local law. Some have even spoken of a process of legal "Anglicization," particularly when referring to the eighteenth century.

A corollary concern of more immediate interest is whether the English Government intended to transfer English law to the colonies and the related issue of what the understanding of the colonists was on this matter. These are difficult questions to sort out. Much confusion continued to surround them right up until the American Revolution. Indeed, the misunderstanding that prevailed on opposite sides of the Atlantic with regard to these issues was a major cause of the Revolution. Americans demanded the legal "rights and liberties of Englishmen," but the English resisted this demand.

The key to the problem lies in the so-called conformity clauses of the colony charters and royal commissions to provincial governors. The paradigmatic charter of 1612 stipulated that the Virginia Company was to have full power to pass laws and

ordinances for the good and welfare of the colony "*so always,
as the same be not contrary to the Laws and Statutes of this
our Realm of England.*" This formula, with only minor variations in wording, was repeated in every subsequent grant of
authority issued by the Crown. What did it mean? Did it imply
the transfer of English law? If so, which laws and which statutes?
Local law as well as common law? General statutes in which the
plantations were not named as well as particular ones in which
they were? Statutes passed before the settlement of America as
well as those enacted afterward?

There were no clear-cut answers to these questions. The Privy
Council, the agency that exercised final authority over colonial
affairs, never settled the issue of the extension of English law
as a matter of legal doctrine. What is clear, however, is that the
English interpreted the conformity clauses as restrictive—with the
Crown holding the authority to decide when the restrictions had
been exceeded. In essence, the Crown could and did use the
conformity clauses as a convenient instrument for striking down
colonial law that was found to be administratively or otherwise
objectionable. The colonists, on the other hand, viewed the conformity clause as the basis for a wholesale reception of the common law, with all its attendant checks on royal discretion. They
claimed the full range of English common-law liberties, limited
only by parliamentary statutes in which the colonies were specifically named.

The closest approximation to settled law on this whole matter
was *Calvin's Case* (also referred to as the *Case of the Postnati*),
decided in the Court of Exchequer Chamber in 1608, at the very
outset of English colonization. The case of one Robert Calvin,
an infant born in Scotland in 1606, after the accession of James I,
was entered in the courts of King's Bench and Chancery and then
removed for hearing by a panel of the most distinguished judges
of the realm. The court held that Scots born after the personal
union of Scotland and England in 1603 were not aliens and
could inherit real property like other subjects of the English
King. But with regard to the new American colonies, the most
relevant portion of the decision, as rendered by Sir Edward
Coke, was the following (7 Coke's Reports 17 [1608]):

> . . . there is a Diversity between a Conquest of a Kingdom of a Christian King, and the Conquest of a Kingdom of an infidel; for if a King come to a Christian Kingdom by Conquest . . . he may at his Pleasure alter and change the Laws of that Kingdom, but until he doth make an Alteration of those Laws, the ancient Laws of that Kingdom remain. But if a Christian King should conquer a Kingdom of an infidel, and bring them under his subjection, then . . . the Laws of the infidel are abrogated, for that they be not only against Christianity, but against the Law of God and of Nature, contained in the Decalogue, and in that Case, until certain Laws be established amongst them, the King by himself, and such Judges as he shall appoint, shall judge them and their Causes according to natural Equity. . . . But if a King hath a Kingdom by Title of Descent . . . he cannot change those Laws of himself, without Consent of Parliament.

Lands outside the realm acquired by the King fell into three categories as regards the law: (1) in lands seized by conquest from a Christian king, existing law remained in force until altered by the new sovereign; (2) in lands taken from infidels, local law was automatically abrogated by the fact of conquest, and the territory came under direct royal governance; (3) in lands acquired by descent, local law could not be changed without the consent of Parliament.

But none of these three conditions of territorial acquisition exactly fitted the circumstances under which England came to settle America. For the most part, the early settlements were established by the peaceful "plantation" of regions that had been sparsely inhabited or, in the case of occupied lands, by purchase from the Indians. Only rarely did acquisition occur through conquest and treaty. Moreover, the automatic application of royal authority to lands acquired by conquest from infidels, as set forth in *Calvin,* hardly pertained to America, since here the question was not what law would govern the Indians but what law would govern migrating Englishmen. Nevertheless, for purposes that suited the English imperial authority, the fiction was maintained that America had been conquered from infidels and, as such, was subject to the royal prerogative. Charter grants, such as that given to Massachusetts, merely affirmed familiar bylaw powers customarily extended to local corporate bodies in England; they in no way diminished the absolute sovereignty of the Crown to govern its overseas plantations.

The use to which the Crown later put *Calvin's Case* is even more curious in view of the fact that, from the early seventeenth century, it was becoming fairly clear that Englishmen in "settled colonies" outside the realm were subject to the jurisdiction of Parliament and, by inference, possessed all the constitutional rights of English citizens. *Calvin's Case* itself suggested that once English law had been introduced, as in Ireland, "no succeeding King could alter the same without Parliament"—dictum that was later to be applied to settled colonies in general. In several cases at the end of the seventeenth century, it was argued that, in settled (as opposed to conquered) territories, English law was in force because English subjects did not surrender their common-law birthright by migrating to distant lands. Parliamentary statutes of 1351 and 1708 specifically entitled subjects born abroad (that is, in lands outside the English realm and dominions) to the rights of Englishmen. It was strange doctrine indeed that gave to Englishmen living in foreign countries more rights in English law than subjects living in colonies to which they had migrated for the greater glory of England.

By the middle of the eighteenth century, the distinction between conquered and settled colonies was clarified in *Campbell* v. *Hall,* where Lord Mansfield held that Englishmen in settled colonies had all the rights of English subjects. As Blackstone put it in his influential *Commentaries* (I, 107):

> . . . if an uninhabited country be discovered and planted by English subjects, all the English laws are immediately there in force. For as the law is the birthright of every subject, so wherever they go they carry their laws with them. But in conquered or ceded countries, that have already laws of their own, the king may indeed alter and change those laws.

Yet, although reality begged for recognition that the English mainland settlements fell more in the category of uninhabited territories to which Englishmen had migrated bearing English law and English rights, the conquered-territory doctrine continued to be applied to America in one of the most interesting and consequential fictions of Anglo-American legal history. Blackstone, citing *Calvin's Case*, continued:

> Our American plantations are principally of this latter sort, being obtained in the last century either by right of conquest and driving out the natives . . . or by treaties. And therefore the common law of England as such has no allowances or authority there; they being no part of the mother country, but distinct (though dependent) dominions.

To this view of things the American colonists demurred. They resisted the implications of *Calvin's Case*, their consequent subjugation to unimpaired royal prerogative, the nonapplicability of certain parliamentary statutes to the colonies, and the prevalent English doctrine that the common law had not been transferred across the sea either by charter grant or by the fact of settlement. Where they could, the Americans disregarded these limits on their legal competence. In civil and criminal litigation not subject to Privy Council review, the American bench and bar simply drew their law from the deep well of English common and statute law. Colonial legislatures adopted parliamentary statutes in name or in substance as needed without worrying about their legal authority to do so, even though such legislative acts were subject to royal disallowance.

But by the time of the Revolution, it was still not clear which elements of English law applied to America. The colonists claimed that American courts and legislatures, not Parliament, the Board of Trade, or the Privy Council, should decide which parts of common and statute law were received in the colonies. England's refusal to accede to these demands and to modify its legal posture contributed to the polarization that led to Independence.

II

As transplanted Englishmen, colonial Americans had a keen sense of those constitutional liberties that were England's pride in the seventeenth and eighteenth centuries. England's legal and constitutional development was living history for Americans. Substantive and procedural guarantees of personal freedom dating back to Magna Carta were standards by which government performance was measured in colonial and Revolutionary America. The transplantation of many of those guarantees can be noted both in formal constitutional documents and in the everyday administration of justice. Indeed, one of the more remarkable achievements of colonial Americans was the significant process of refinement that some of those guarantees underwent in the course of their migration across the Atlantic. Such guarantees were part of the written law of every colony in America by 1701. New England, the Middle Atlantic provinces, and the South— royal, proprietary, and charter colonies alike—all reflected a lively appreciation of the English constitutional tradition. This formal recognition can easily be documented, but for purposes of illustration it is necessary only to point to a few leading examples.

In 1637–38, the first Maryland General Assembly passed an act "for the liberties of the people" that, as re-enacted the following year, stated that the individual safeguards embedded in the English common law were to be the rights of Marylanders as well as Englishmen:

> . . . that all the Inhabitants of this Province being Christians (slaves excepted) shall have and enjoy all such rights liberties immunities priviledges and free customs within this Province as any naturall born subject of England hath or ought to have or enjoy in the Realm of England by force or vertue of the common law or Statute Law of England. . . . And shall not be imprisoned nor disseissed or dispossessed of their freehold goods or Chattels or be out Lawed Exiled or otherwise destroyed fore judged or punished then according to the Laws of this province.

As we have seen, the whole question of whether such references to the common and statutory law of England constituted formal reception of English law is a complicated one. What is at least evident from this early legislative enactment is that the freemen of the Calvert proprietorship desired to establish the basic common-law protections usually subsumed under what was later referred to as "due process of law" and thereby to create in Maryland a legal environment attractive to prospective settlers. Indeed, despite legal dubiety, the references to the "liberties, franchises, and immunities" of freeborn English subjects that were included, with only minor modifications, in all the original colonial charters served to advertise overseas adventure and the planting of English settlements.

But the leading example of the effort to establish basic rights in the early period of colonial settlement occurred in Massachusetts. The *Body of Liberties* of 1641 was enacted in response to growing fears that the magistracy of the Bay Colony was becoming a domineering oligarchy. More a "compilation of constitutional provisions" (Haskins, 1960: 129) than a written code of laws, the *Body of Liberties* was designed to keep the tendency toward arbitrary rule in check. Nathaniel Ward, its principal draftsman, was one of the few men in Massachusetts with legal training, so that, while the code contained Mosaic provisions responsive to the colony's religious orientation, its detailed enumeration of civil liberties reflects Ward's substantial common-law background as well as English legal culture in general.

There are numerous concordances between the *Body of Liberties* and English common law. In fact, to answer complaints that local law did not conform sufficiently to English law, the General Court later issued the Declaration of 1646—a parallel listing of the "common lawes and customes of England, beginning with Magna Carta," on one side, and, on the other, the "summe of such lawes and customes as are in force and use in this jurisdiction." For its own political purposes, the General Court exaggerated the degree of coincidence between the two bodies of law. Still, many were clearly rooted in the English tradition. Of none was this more true than Liberty 1:

> No mans life shall be taken away, no mans honour or good name shall be stayned, no mans person shall be arested, restrayned, banished, dismembred, nor any wayes punished, no man shall be deprived of his wife or children, no mans goods or estaite shall be taken away from him, nor any way indammaged under colour of law or Countenance of Authoritie, unlesse it be by vertue or

equitie of some expresse law of the Country waranting the same, established by a generall Court and sufficiently published.

While the phrase "due process of law" does not appear in this first and most important provision of the *Body of Liberties,* it was close enough to the famous "law of the land" section 39 of Magna Carta to demonstrate a conscious effort at duplication: "No free man shall be taken, imprisoned, disseised, outlawed, banished, or in any way destroyed, nor will We proceed against or prosecute him, except by the lawful judgment of his peers and by the law of the land."

Other provisions of the *Body of Liberties* also reflected English common law: the right to equal justice (Liberty 2), the right to fair trial by jury (Liberties 29 and 30), and the guarantees against the use of cruel and barbarous punishments (Liberty 46). But more significant than these rough approximations between the *Body of Liberties* and the fundamentals of the common law were the refinements, improvements, and innovations with which the Puritans worked over their legal heritage: Aliens as well as inhabitants were to enjoy equal justice; bail was less restricted than in England; jurors were free to follow their consciences in reaching a just verdict and were not to be intimidated by threats of fine or imprisonment by the court as in England; appeal was granted as of right in capital cases and was not restricted to review of trial-court procedural errors granted at the discretion of the appellate body; double jeopardy extended to civil and criminal cases alike and was not, as in England, limited to capital offenses; and, finally, the right to confront witnesses and accusers was, in Massachusetts, absolute in capital cases and more extensive in noncapital cases than it was in England, where written depositions were normally accepted in evidence in felony trials. In addition, no man was required to fight in offensive wars beyond the borders of the province but only in defensive wars (Liberty 7); all inhabitants—freeman and foreigner alike— were able to participate in public deliberations such as town meetings (Liberty 12); the right to travel freely was recognized (Liberty 17); the right to counsel was guaranteed without restriction as to the nature of the offense (Liberty 26); a minimum of two witnesses was required for conviction in capital cases (Liberty 47); and jurors were to be chosen by the freemen of the town (Liberty 50). All these provisions of the *Body of Liberties* added up to a program of genuine legal reform.

The experiment in written constitutionalism that began with the Bay Colony's charter itself and continued with the *Body of Liberties*—a kind of early Bill of Rights—reached its culmination with the *Laws and Liberties* of 1648: the "first modern code of the Western world" (Haskins:120), a model for legal draftsmen in other colonies, and the basic law of Massachusetts until the abrogation of the original charter in 1684. The *Laws and Liberties* carried forward the tradition of reform already established in the earlier legislation of the 1640's. The basic freedoms adumbrated in the *Body of Liberties* were detailed at greater length. Moreover, as a code of fundamental law, the *Laws and Liberties* were designed to limit the discretion of legislators and magistrates to fixed principles—an idea that was to reach fulfillment and conceptual clarity only in the constitutional period in the latter part of the eighteenth century. The basic rights that formed so essential a part of this legislation raised them to a higher level of constitutional significance. In that respect, the Massachusetts code of 1648 sounded the note that was to be struck repeatedly in the seventeenth century, one that would resonate many years later in the Antifederalist claim that a constitution without basic liberties was not a constitution at all.

Both the Maryland law of 1638, which projected a reception of English liberties by general reference, and the Massachusetts legislation of the 1640's represent initiatives taken by freemen and their deputies to establish popular safeguards against arbitrary rule. A generation later, however, we find similar regard for constitutional rights, which, somewhat surprisingly, was undertaken at the instance not of those "below" but of those "above." The *Concessions and Agreements of West New Jersey* (1676–77) was authored by Edward Byllynge, the purchaser of the Berkeley proprietary interest in West Jersey, with the collaboration of William Penn, one of the managers of Byllynge's affairs. Like the earlier *Concessions and Agreements* of 1664–65, issued by Berkeley and Carteret, the original grantees of the

Province of New Jersey, the Byllynge-Penn version was designed
to promote settlement by offering generous conditions to immigrants. But unlike the Berkeley-Carteret *Concessions,* the fundamental laws of 1676-77 were animated by the same spirit of
liberalism that would later generate William Penn's *Frame of
Government* for Pennsylvania in 1683. In both instances—that
of West New Jersey and that of Pennsylvania—we find the establishment of a high standard of constitutionalism as measured by
guarantees of individual liberty resulting from the convictions
of a small group of high-minded men determined to establish
in America a home for English liberties that was impossible to
achieve in England itself.

The *Concessions and Agreements of West New Jersey* is a
precedent for American constitutionalism in three important
respects: First, it vested the power of self-government in the
inhabitants of the province through the establishment of a general assembly of deputies chosen in free and democratic elections and exercising full legislative competence (Chaps. 32-44).

Second, it secured basic guarantees of civil liberty: freedom
of conscience and of worship (Chap. 16); no deprivation of life,
liberty, or estate but by lawful judgment of twelve jurymen,
with the accused having an absolute right to thirty-five peremptory challenges and an unlimited right to challenge for cause
(Chap. 17); in all offenses excepting felony and treason, every
inhabitant was entitled to notice by official summons stating the
cause, the identity of the accusers, and the court of hearing at
least fourteen days prior to appearance, such notification to pre-
cede any subsequent process for arrest, attachment, or imprisonment (Chap. 18); the judgment of the jury was not subject to
court reversal (Chap. 19); two witnesses were required for conviction in civil and criminal causes (Chap. 20); no person was
obliged to employ counsel but could plead his own cause (Chap.
22); and all trials were to be public, "that Justice may not be
done in a corner nor in any Covert manner [and] that all and
every person and persons Inhabiting the said Province shall as
farr as in us lies be free from oppression and slavery" (Chap. 23).

Third, the *Concessions and Agreements* set forth the principle
of the fundamentality of a written constitution as opposed to
ordinary statutory legislation, a distinction implied in the Mas-

sachusetts codes but articulated with philosophic and stylistic precision in West New Jersey. Chapter 13 spelled out this understanding with remarkable clarity:

> That the common Law or fundamental Rights and priviledges of West New Jersey are Individually agreed upon by the Proprietors and freeholders thereof to be the foundation of the Government which is not to be altered by the Legislative Authority or free Assembly hereafter mentioned and constituted[.] But that the said Legislative Authority is constituted according to these fundamentalls to make such Laws as agree with and maintaine the said fundamentalls and to make no Laws that in the least contrast differ or vary from the said fundamentalls under what pretence or allegation soever.

Members of the Assembly who willfully attempted to "move or excite any to move" legislation subversive of these fundamentals were to be proceeded against as "traitors to the said Government." Finally, this "great Charter of fundamentalls" was to be read at the opening and at the dissolution of every General Assembly and four times a year in the courts of justice.

A century later, at the time of the American Revolution, the distinction between fundamental and statutory law would achieve institutional expression in the "convention"; an assembly of the representatives of the "people out of doors" (Wood, 1969: chap. 8), organized for the sole purpose of devising a framework of government and a list of constitutional rights untouchable by ordinary lawmakers. The *West New Jersey Concessions and Agreements* anticipated this development. Although it was drafted by the chief proprietor and his agent, it was adopted by the mutual consent and agreement of proprietors, freeholders, and inhabitants. It lodged genuine sovereign power in the people's representatives, limited only by the guarantees of the basic charter itself. "In every sense [it] was a true constitution" (Boyd, 1964:14).

Other examples of charter rights abounded in early America. Some approached the elaboration of the Massachusetts codes and the New Jersey charter. Such was the case in Pennsylvania, where the "Laws agreed upon in England," adopted in May, 1682, provided for the full panoply of civil liberties—one of the hall-

marks of William Penn's "Holy Experiment." Technically not a
part of the Pennsylvania "frame of government," this early legislation was considered to be as fundamental as the charter itself
and survived the subsequent modifications of the Pennsylvania
constitution in 1701. Elsewhere, only particular concerns received
emphasis. The Rhode Island royal charter of 1663, for example,
secured the "free exercise and enjoyment of all civil and religious
rights" and to that end guaranteed "that noe person within the
sayd colony . . . shall bee any wise molested, punished, disquieted,
or called in question, for any differences in opinione in matters
of religion." Other civil liberties received the customary scanty
formula assurance of the "libertyes and immunityes of ffree and
naturall subjects . . . of England."

New York's *Charter of Libertyes,* enacted by the first General
Assembly of that province in 1683 (and subsequently repudiated
by the Privy Council), claimed rights and privileges that no other
English colony possessed: not only jury trial, bail, and the other
elements of due process, but freedom from taxation without representation, liberty of conscience, protection against the quarter-
ing of troops or the imposition of martial law, and, finally, the
establishment of a provincial legislature virtually equal in sovereign power to Parliament itself. Such local pretensions to independence and civil liberty invited disallowance, particularly at
a time when the last of the Stuart monarchs was attempting to
consolidate his imperial dominions while increasing the power
of the royal prerogative in the colonial sphere. Still, the *Charter
of Liberties* is a paradigmatic case illustrating colonial claims to
English liberty. While the charter itself did not remain in force
for very long, its civil-libertarian provisions, especially those regarding criminal process, were re-enacted in subsequent legislation and were adopted as standards for the administration of
justice.

Finally, at the opening of the eighteenth century, one of the
greatest expressions of the colonial mind—Pennsylvania's *Charter
of Privileges* of 1701—implanted a system of government and a
standard of official performance unsurpassed for its constitutional
liberalism either in England or in America. Not so detailed as
the Massachusetts *Laws and Liberties* of 1648 nor even so extensive as the New Jersey *Concessions and Agreements* of 1677, the

Pennsylvania charter had the simplicity and economy of later state constitutions. It extended the detailed legal guarantees of 1683 in several important particulars: for example, in guaranteeing to the accused in criminal trials the right to summon witnesess and to have them testify under oath and the right to counsel. Moreover, Article VIII clearly established the fundamentality of the charter by providing that "no Act, Law or Ordinance whatsoever, shall at any time hereafter, be made or done, to alter, change or diminish the Form or Effect of this charter . . . without the Consent of the Governor . . . and *Six* Parts of *Seven* of the Assembly." Any laws passed contrary to its provisions were to be of no force or effect.

Despite variations in emphasis, elaborateness, or philosophical clarity, it is fair to say that, by the end of the seventeenth century, the American constitutional experience—as reflected in royal charters and concessions handed down by the Crown or by the proprietors of royal grants as well as in legislation initiated from below by the people's deputies—recognized the central importance of legal guarantees of personal liberty secured by some kind of written enactment whose authority was beyond ordinary statutory control. A diverse assortment of civil liberties, from the ancient right to jury trial to the new recognition of freedom of conscience, had won formal endorsement in many of the mainland colonies that would later become the United States. The Pennsylvania *Charter of Privileges* was the basis of government in that province until the Revolution, but it may also be interpreted as a kind of summary statement of the seventeenth-century colonial constitutional experience. That experience had seen the adoption of written instruments containing minimal standards for local and imperial authorities to follow. This in itself was a remarkable achievement. It meant that, at their very inception, American political societies gave recognition to the more liberal and forward-looking elements in the English legal tradition.

III

But the American colonial experience went further. Not only in form but in substance and practice as well, the American colonies endeavored to achieve, and in many places did achieve, a record of performance that legitimized, perpetuated, and advanced the English constitutional tradition more than basic legislative enactments and even corporate charters could ever do. The record of this performance is to be found not only in the acts of colonial legislatures loftily claiming the rights of Englishmen but in the everyday workings of the judicial system, particularly in the sphere of criminal-law enforcement. It is in this area—where the individual confronts the weight and power of the state—that the true measure of constitutionalism can be taken.

The record of the American colonies is not uniform. From one province to another and even within a single colony, the pattern of judicial administration varied from the frontier counties, where legal knowledge was thin, to the capital city, where the trained bar congregated. Even so, recent studies of county courts in colonial America show surprisingly high levels of judicial administration in fairly remote settlements, with procedures comparable in efficiency and sophistication to more established regions and to local law enforcement in England itself. The higher the degree of judicial refinement, the greater the likelihood that Americans enjoyed the benefits of "due process of law."

The phrase "due process of law" has had a long and honored career in Anglo-American legal history. Its reservoirs of "residual meaning" have given it renewed life in every major era of constitutional development, so that it defies easy definition. It implies that all authority must act according to law—"that there is no sovereign unless he conforms to the principles of legality" (Mott, 1926: 589)—a general definition with wide ramifications. At the very minimum, however, "due process," particularly in the colonial period of our history, meant the employment of proper forms of indictment, notice, hearing, and trial. In America, due process did not become a great rallying principle until the Revolution, but the colonists did expect courts of law and law officers to follow appropriate procedures. This was the basic standard governing the administration of justice—a standard, interestingly enough, which judges, lawyers, and prosecutors upheld as a matter of professional obligation as much as laymen demanded it as a matter of high principle.

The legal history of colonial New York illustrates the extent to which due process of law was recognized in pre-Revolutionary America. In some ways, New York no more than equaled contemporary English procedures in safeguarding the rights of individuals caught up in the machinery of criminal justice. This was particularly true in the field of "summary process," the trial of persons accused of crime before judges without juries. Both in England and in America, social conditions necessitated summary procedures. The problem of vagabondage and petty crime was serious and growing in the eighteenth century. Faced with the costs of detaining and trying the vagrant poor, legislatures resorted to the expedient of increasing the number of offenses that were subject to summary process. The result was that, while great constitutional importance was attached to the formal procedures of accusation by grand jury and trial by petit jury, the bulk of criminal offenders were, in effect, dealt with administratively before a single magistrate.

The wide use of summary process was probably inevitable, given the growth of social unrest in the late colonial period, but it certainly vitiated the high-sounding claims to constitutional liberty—in particular the inviolability of the jury—that colonial New Yorkers were to continue to make right up to the Revolution. The precedents for the use of summary procedures were well established in England, where justices of the peace and local committing magistrates traditionally exercised such powers in criminal-law enforcement. Nevertheless, the duplication of this precedent in New York (and elsewhere), however punctilious the colonists may have become in insisting that magistrates adhere to regular procedures as set forth in the leading handbooks, such as Dalton's *Countrey Justice,* meant that, in this important area of law enforcement, the Americans did not progress much beyond the administrative practices customary in England.

In other ways, however, Americans did improve on English practice in protecting individual liberties. In English common law, defendants were not permitted the benefit of counsel in felony cases. Counsel, if present, could not cross-examine witnesses or address the jury but could only raise legal points for the consideration of the court. Given the low state of development of the law of evidence, however, this was of little consequence in most trials, even where defendants could afford legal counsel.

Some of the mainland colonies followed the English practice in this regard. For example, the very fact that New York more nearly duplicated English practice than most other provinces meant that the less desirable features of common law—such as the deprivation of counsel—were in force there. Elsewhere, however, such was not the case. Rhode Island, in 1669, permitted the employment of defense counsel in all cases. In Connecticut, it is not altogether clear when the received law was reformed in this area, but in the 1790's Zephaniah Swift, an early court reporter, noted that "we have never admitted [in Connecticut] that cruel and illiberal principle of the common law of England that when a man is on trial for his life, he shall be refused counsel, and denied those means of defence, which are allowed, when the most trifling pittance of property is in question." The Pennsylvania *Charter of Privileges* of 1701 (also in force in Delaware) specifically provided that "all criminals shall have the same Privileges of Witnesses and Council as their Prosecutors," and a 1718 Pennsylvania statute required the assignment of counsel in capital cases as well as witness process for those accused of crime. In 1701, the Massachusetts General Court provided for counsel in criminal as well as civil cases. In general, Massachusetts courts assigned counsel for needy defendants in murder cases. A Virginia law of 1734 allowed defense counsel in capital cases but did not permit cross-examination or address to the jury. South Carolina in 1731 provided for the assignment of counsel at the request of the accused, since, in the words of the statute, "many innocent persons under criminal prosecutions, may suffer for want of knowledge in the laws, how to make a just defence . . . for which reasons [they] ought to have proper assistance, and all just and equal means allowed them to defend their innocencies." In short, in about half of the original Thirteen Colonies, counsel was permitted in felony cases long before the Revolution, although in all probability most criminal defendants could not afford the advantage of a trained attorney, and only in Massachusetts, Pennsylvania, and South Carolina was counsel assigned. But by the time of the formation of the federal Constitution, the right to counsel was established in the fundamental law of nearly every state, including New York—a significant advance over the English practice, where the right to a full defense by legal counsel in felony trials was not recognized by statute until 1836.

Innovations on English practice occurred in other areas as well. The grand jury of accusation began as an instrument of royal justice in the days of the Norman kings, but in the course of its evolution it had become a popular check upon the royal prerogative. The grand jury protected the citizen from unfounded accusation. By the seventeenth century, however, the English grand jury was becoming more an arm of the state and less a popular defense against arbitrary power—similar in some ways to the American grand jury today.

In colonial America, the grand jury—where it was used—achieved much greater independence and autonomy than its English counterpart. The absence of a regular constabulary meant that individual grand jurors assumed the responsibility for presenting criminal offenders. There are instances of colonial grand juries hearing evidence for the defense, whereas in England only King's evidence was admissible. Jurymen were not always chosen by the county sheriff, as in England, but sometimes by local bodies, such as the courts or town meetings. Property qualifications for grand-jury service were not high (except in the Carolinas), so that grand jurymen were drawn from a wider social group, and jury duty was not strictly confined to the wealthy few. In New England towns grand-jury service was rotated among the free inhabitants. Grand juries took on many local administrative functions: They reported on road conditions, investigated official performance, passed local ordinances. It was, in fact, a representative institution of local government, a kind of "county parliament" (Stephen, 1883:I, 253).

In the field of criminal-law enforcement, there was a widespread belief that accusation by grand jury was the only acceptable means of initiating proceedings against criminal offenders. Maryland, in 1715, prohibited accusation by any other means, and in 1727 a committee of the South Carolina legislature opposed the *information*, a method of accusation by the prosecutor acting alone. Most notably New York, also in 1727, in an act subsequently disallowed by the Privy Council, barred accusations by information. Moreover, except in the South, grand juries were reluctant to approve the *bill of indictment* customarily prepared in advance for the grand jury by the prosecution; they preferred the *presentment,* a formal accusation initiated and drawn by the grand jury itself. This preference was evidence of the tendency of some American grand juries to revert to medieval English practice, in which the grand jury was a genuine investigatory body, or "inquest," of citizens. The New York experience illustrates an attitude widespread in colonial America, that the grand jury was an important defense of individual liberty and a check on Crown officers, prosecuting attorneys in particular. Through the grand jury, the power to prosecute was curbed, and this had a major impact on the government's ability to enforce seditious-libel laws or violations of the Acts of Trade.

As a consequence, the Crown resorted to the information in proceeding against law violators, although the records indicate that, even in New York, it was used less frequently than in England. In addition, the *qui tam* action—a civil action brought by a private informer suing for a breach of some statute who then shares the penalties with the government—was a device employed by the Crown to enforce the provisions of the Navigation Acts without having to go before the local grand jury for an indictment. Oddly enough, there seems to have been less objection on constitutional grounds to *qui tam* proceedings —often employed in summary process—than there was to the Crown information.

In other ways, American legal practice achieved a level of performance on a par with English procedure. The right against compulsory self-incrimination—one of the focal points of the constitutional debates of the Stuart period—was recognized in England by the middle of the seventeenth century. It emerged out of the struggle between the state and individuals accused of public crimes, such as treason, sedition, and heresy, but, by the end of the seventeenth century, it was being applied to defendants in ordinary criminal proceedings. Like other common-law liberties, however, this right was not automatically transferred to the American colonies. It was a right that "had to win its way to recognition in every colony" (Levy, 1968:334). While the record indicates that America lagged behind England on the right against self-incrimination in the early period, by the time of the Revolution it had achieved nearly universal acceptance in the colonies.

The right of a defendant not to be compelled to give evidence against himself was manifested in a number of ways: The accused could be questioned but not under oath during preliminary examination; witnesses could not be compelled to incriminate themselves when giving evidence against others; oaths of purgation, in which a failure to swear one's innocence of a statutory violation was prima facie evidence of guilt, were gradually dropped from legislative enactments.

To be sure, the right against self-incrimination was not, in the eighteenth century, what it was to become in the twentieth century. Nowadays, the accused must be apprised of his right to say nothing to the police, and coerced confessions are inadmissible in evidence. But two hundred years ago the right not to incriminate oneself had to be claimed. The state had no obligation to advise the prisoner that he might remain silent. Confessions, usually elicited by intimidation ("close examination"), though unsworn, were admitted in evidence at trial. If the accused challenged his pretrial admissions, he opened himself to questioning by the court and comment by the prosecutor. In fact, the admissibility of confessions often led to conviction in a summary proceeding, and this in itself denied the most important element of due process—the right to a jury trial. For the poor and ignorant offender, unaided by legal counsel, the right against compulsory self-incrimination was often an empty and meaningless constitutional liberty. Still, to the extent that it was available for those who were knowledgeable enough to demand it, the right against compulsory self-incrimination was a part of American liberty in the late colonial period.

So was the privilege of *habeas corpus ad subjiciendum*—the right of an individual confined by the authorities to a court inquiry into the cause of his confinement. Whether or not the privilege of the writ of habeas corpus, the "most celebrated writ in English Law" (Blackstone:III, 129), was in force in the colonies involved the larger question of the transference of parliamentary statutes—in particular, the Habeas Corpus Act of 1679. The Act itself did not establish the privilege; it merely regulated and improved the procedures governing its enforcement in England. The accepted doctrine was that, since the colonies were not named in the Act, it did not apply. Efforts by individual colonies to adopt the 1679 statute in name or in substance by legislative enactment met disallowance by the King in Council. Nevertheless, the right to habeas corpus was widely recognized in fact by colonial courts. The writ was part of the common law to which the colonists believed they were entitled. In most provinces, the threat of royal disallowance prevented formal reception of the Habeas Corpus Act, but the privilege was known and implemented in most of the colonies and was allowed to exist with only intermittent interference from royal authorities.

As late as the eighteenth century, the English common-law criminal trial was but a dim foreshadowing of modern trial procedure. The criminal defendant could not see the indictment. There was no pretrial discovery of the prosecution's evidence. Counsel was barred in felony cases, on the theory that innocence needed no defense and that the criminal law was simple enough to comprehend, so that the average defendant needed no technical legal knowledge in order to prove his defense. The jury trial was, in concept at least, a kind of gladiatorial combat between equal contestants, with the court sitting as a neutral referee, alert to infringements on the accused's legal rights.

In fact, however, the whole procedure was weighted in favor of the prosecution. Rules of evidence were rudimentary, and little was excluded on grounds of inadmissibility. Written depositions could be read in evidence without the chance for rebuttal or cross-examination of absent witnesses. Defendant confessions, exacted by intimidation in pretrial proceedings, were admissible at trial. Finally, juries were deprived of creature comforts during deliberation and were virtually coerced into rendering guilty verdicts.

In general, New York followed English trial practices. In

felony cases, counsel could intercede only on points of law, although—again, as in England—in misdemeanor and treason trials, counsel could conduct a full defense. Jury panels, however, were selected impartially. The right to challenge for cause was recognized, although, in the absence of defense counsel, it was seldom used. Juries resisted directed verdicts and found special or general verdicts as their consciences—not the court—dictated. For the most part, jury trials—when conducted—were fair. The sanctity and finality of the trial jury's verdict were upheld as a basic constitutional principle, and this seems to have been recognized by the government and the courts. When Lieutenant Governor Cadwallader Colden challenged this well-established tradition in the middle 1760's, he raised a clamor as loud as the protest against the Stamp Act itself. Trials were speedy because of the likelihood that defendants in custody would escape, and also because it was costly for all concerned to drag out the proceedings. In the eighteenth century, however, there was a growing recognition of defendants' right to postponement—part of the general expansion of the rights of the accused in the Age of Enlightenment.

Defendants in felony cases were hurt by limited subpoena privileges, arbitrary court decisions on whether or not defense witnesses could be sworn, the admissibility of hearsay evidence, secrecy surrounding the indictment, and defendants' inability to confront their accusers at preliminary hearings. On the other hand, juries often sided with the accused when the prosecution was upholding Crown interests; the burden of proof was on the shoulders of the state; written depositions were allowed only in misdemeanor trials after 1750; and at summary trials defendants were allowed to cross-examine. Thus, despite the English standard, and despite all the impediments strewn in the path of the accused, the records indicate a large number of acquittals in jury trials. In the end, the conduct of trials was no more oppressive in New York than in contemporary England and probably much less so, given the greater independence of juries plus the popular hostility to the Crown, which New York juries both reflected and represented.

Measured by court practices, the precise meaning of "due

process of law" varied considerably from one colony to another. Even within a single province, judicial practice went through marked transformations from the seventeenth to the eighteenth century. As a result, it is difficult to make accurate generalizations regarding the colonial experience as a whole. Nevertheless, certain tendencies are apparent in the development of colonial law. There was a decided movement toward the "Anglicization" of American law as the colonial period advanced. As the bench and the bar became better trained and more knowledgeable, and as the written sources of law became more available, colonial law moved closer to the English model. The result was a growing attention to procedural exactitude and increasing awareness of the importance of proper form. Moreover, the tension between English common law and seventeenth-century colonial law gave American law a certain dynamic thrust, which pushed it in the direction of change. Indeed, while the English standard was the goal, where American procedure had improved upon it—as in the early recognition and widespread implementation of the right to counsel in felony cases or the somewhat greater emphasis upon oral evidence at trial—those advances were preserved, thus imparting to the American legal tradition a reformist character that was one of the singular and lasting achievements of the colonial period.

IV

Thus, the legal experience of early America suggests that the attempt to establish English law and the "rights and liberties of Englishmen" was constant from the first settlements to the Revolution. There were, of course, important exceptions. Everywhere in America, slaves were treated differently. Special courts were set up to deal with crimes committed by slaves. Grand-jury presentment was usually abandoned where slaves were concerned, and trial by a panel of judges took the place of trial by a jury of laymen. On the other hand, out of solicitude for their masters, slaves were sometimes permitted, in felony cases, to have an attorney—usually their owner—in places where legal counsel was normally barred. In addition, although statutory penalties

for black slaves were usually more severe than for whites con-
victed of the same crime, since slaves were valued as property,
mitigation of sentence was fairly frequent. Finally, while regular
due process was dispensed with, there was a feeling that, even
in cases involving slaves, some regularity of procedure should
prevail.

Bonded servants also received modified treatment in court. In
Virginia, for example, the jury panel in cases involving indentured servants could be drawn entirely from the bystanders at
court rather than from residents of the vicinity of the crime.
When servants were the petitioners in court, their complaints
were usually handled informally rather than by regular process.
And they were excluded from jury service—a proscription that
seriously impaired their ability to achieve equal justice. But
white servants also possessed certain rights in law: The terms of
their contracts were enforceable in the courts; statutes protected
them from cruel and inhuman treatment; and servant testimony
was accepted in evidence even in cases between master and
servant.

In general, the bias inherent in a judicial system in which
local magistrates and judges were recruited from the propertied
classes while the poor, the vagabond, the semi-free and the slave
were all subject to summary or informal process undercut the
chances of equal treatment for all before the law. The legal disabilities facing these groups help to define the limits of civil
liberty in colonial America. Nevertheless, measured by the eighteenth century rather than the twentieth, colonial Americans
were in the forefront of legal reform and in the process of
broadening and redefining the meaning of due process of law.
English common law was thought to be the closest approximation to justice that mankind had ever achieved. The colonists
resented the accepted English doctrine, which withheld that law
from them; they disregarded it where they could; and after 1760,
they resisted, even to revolution, imperial attempts to enforce it.
Above all, the Americans were determined to create a system of
law that was responsive to their needs and experience as well
as to their English heritage. The results, while uneven, point to
a consistent effort to implement in fact what early charters,

codes, and basic statutes of fundamental law had set forth with simple clarity and liberal zeal. Constitutional guarantees of personal liberty were at least as secure in colonial America as in England and in some respects even more so.

4

The Relations Between Church
and State

I

The single-church establishment was the familiar cultural mold
that shaped the thinking and set the course for the first European
settlers in America. Under this system of close state-church cooperation, a single religious body, usually encompassing a majority of the population, enjoyed special legal privileges and
protections. Competing religious institutions and doctrines were
suppressed, either directly or indirectly; tax monies for the support of the church were collected by the state; the establishment
ran whatever schools and colleges there were; church officials
administered welfare and charity; and the crucial events of individual and family life—birth, marriage, divorce, and death—were
regulated by the deeds and punctuated by the ceremonies of the
standing ecclesiastical order. Above all, an orthodox constella-
tion of beliefs was rigidly enforced by the vigorous application
of criminal statutes against heresy, blasphemy, and idolatry.

State power was a major instrument working toward the
achievement of uniformity of faith and worship. True religion,
said Nathaniel Ward in 1645, "strictly binds every Conscience
to contend earnestly for the Truth: to preserve unity of Spirit,
Faith and Ordinances, to be all like minded, of one accord; every
man to take his Brother into his Christian care, to stand fast with

one spirit, with one mind, striving together for the faith of the Gospel; and by no means to permit Heresies or Erronious Opinions" *(The Simple Cobler of Aggawam,* 1645). Church and state were allied institutions in the common struggle to re-create well-ordered polities in a wilderness environment.

But the American climate was hostile to traditional patterns of church-state relations. The very conditions of American life, the necessities of settlement, and the character of the immigrant population eroded traditions set in granite and replaced them with notions, attitudes, and practices that pointed in new directions. The idea that church and state best served society when they rotated in separate and distinct spheres was not widely accepted until after the Revolution, but tendencies of that kind were set in motion in the very beginning by the realities of American colonial life.

First, there was the brute fact of sheer size. As Paul Freund put it, in the Burton Lecture (1965), religious liberty in America is a "function . . . of geographic spaciousness." Provincial America's greatest problem was its need for people, to fill up space, to supply labor, and to develop the country—all in order to advance the chief end of colonization: to increase the wealth and power of the English empire. Religious exclusivity did not square with such goals. For example, Lord Calvert instructed Maryland's Roman Catholics to be tolerant of Protestants. The colony was established as a Catholic refuge but its principal aim was to become a profitable enterprise. Yet, since the proprietor's coreligionists were not expected to emigrate to America in great numbers, Maryland had to be hospitable to the larger number of Protestants who would. Consequently, the Act of Toleration (1649)—that great emblem of early religious liberty—"was neither a Catholic nor a Protestant measure" (Sweet, 1935:48–49), nor was it a product of the liberalism of theory. Rather, it was a simple, practical device for making Maryland attractive to settlers of nearly every Christian persuasion:

> . . . And whereas the inforceing of the conscience in matters of Religion hath frequently fallen out to be of dangerous Consequence in those commonwealthes where it hath been practised,

And for the more quiett and peaceable government of this Province, and the better to preserve mutuall Love and amity amongst the Inhabitants thereof. Be it Therefore . . . enacted . . . that noe person or persons whatsoever within this Province . . . professing to beleive in Jesus Christ, shall from henceforth bee any waies troubled, Molested or discountenanced for or in respect of his or her religion nor in the free exercise thereof . . . nor any way compelled to the beleife or exercise of any other Religion against his or her consent.

Similarly, in the case of Pennsylvania, William Penn's liberalism of principle happened to coincide with the needs of state: His easy land-grant policy, the liberality of his "frames of government," and particularly his toleration of non-Quakers made Pennsylvania the home of a motley assortment of national and religious groups who, together, contributed to the peopling of the province.

Indeed, when individual colonies became too zealous in their pursuit of spiritual uniformity, the English Government struck them down for discouraging settlement. Thus, when, early in the eighteenth century, South Carolina excluded dissenters from sitting in the provincial assembly and tried to establish an Anglican ecclesiastical court, the Privy Council quashed these efforts because they were likely to depopulate the province. In 1750, when the Virginia Council tried to limit the activities of dissenter preachers, the Lords of Trade advised that a "free Exercise of Religion is so valuable a branch of true liberty, and so essential to the enriching and improving of a Trading Nation, it should ever be held sacred in His Majesty's Colonies."

Geographic spaciousness had other consequences for the religious establishment. The openness of the land weakened the hold that churches could exercise through customary procedures of discipline and control. The imposition of strict orthodoxy led to seepage at the edges—of those for whom the prevailing orthodoxy was too conservative, and of others for whom it was too easy-going. In England, the seepage was "vertical"; the heterodox went underground into secret "gatherings" and "conventicles." In America, they moved away by voluntary exile or through punitive banishment. Rhode Island, on the one hand, and the towns

of the Connecticut Valley, on the other, spun off from the orthodoxy of Massachusetts, which was too narrow for the followers of
Roger Williams and too broad for men like Thomas Hooker.
Thus, the American pattern of "horizontal" exit from the church
created competing religious communities that, in time, would
shorten the reach of the "standing order." Similarly, the distances between the colonial branches and the European stock
made the provincial churches separate in fact if not in faith, made
discipline from the center impossible to impose, made kindred
churches within the provinces into semi-autonomous bodies, and
made interprovincial denominational associations an eighteenth-
century necessity to compensate for the processes of fragmentation that had already set in. These new spatial relations had a
revolutionary impact upon the traditional associations of church
and society.

But geography was not the only agent contributing to a breakdown of the single-church establishment model. Reinforcing the
trend toward provincial liberalization was the development of a
religious settlement between the establishment and the nonconforming churches in England itself. By the end of the seventeenth
century, the great waves of political unrest stirred into motion
by the conflict between King and Parliament, Cavalier and
Roundhead, and Anglican and "Puritan" were subsiding. In
1689, Parliament passed the Act of Toleration, which authorized
dissenting sects to hold religious services in public. Catholics as
well as anti-Trinitarians were excluded from the benefits of the
Act, tests for office persisted, and dissenters were still saddled with
civil disabilities. But the Toleration Act, a major component of
the new constitutional order that emerged in the aftermath of
the Bloodless Revolution, contributed to the expansion of religious freedom in America.

The Act was the basis for successful claims in several cases
where itinerant preachers had been denied licenses or prosecuted
for conducting religious services without authorization. More importantly, the Act meant that imperial policy now frowned upon
colonial measures directed against minority churches. The Board
of Trade and the Privy Council implemented this policy on
repeated occasions. In the fall of 1705, the Council disallowed a
Connecticut anti-Quaker statute because it violated the rights of

dissenters now protected by English law. A year later, the Council voided the South Carolina enactment setting up religious tests for office and an ecclesiastical court because these measures were repugnant "to the laws of this realm, and destructive to the constitution of the Church of England."

The Massachusetts Charter of 1691 explicitly stated that "for the greater Ease and Encouragement of Our Loveing Subjects Inhabiting our said Province or Territory of the Massachusetts Bay . . . Wee doe . . . Grant Establish and Ordaine that for ever hereafter there shall be a liberty of Conscience allowed in the Worshipp of God to all Christians (Except Papists)." In addition, the charter substituted a property requirement for the religious test of the old Bay Colony. In this case, the new constitutional provisions benefited Massachusetts Anglicans, the religious minority that the royal government was bound to view with special favor. Still, the application of the Toleration Act even to colonies *with* an Anglican establishment suggests that more than the well-being of a favored group was at stake: The policy of toleration was applied to the American provinces because nothing less than the ultimate success of the colonial enterprise itself was at issue. At least for Protestants, the English Religious Settlement hastened the development of a multiplicity of churches where not too long before the uniformity of worship had been the ideal.

II

By the end of the seventeenth century, there was widespread recognition of freedom of conscience in provincial America. Not surprisingly, Rhode Island's charter of 1663 declared that "everye person and persons may, from tyme to tyme, and at all tymes hereafter, freelye and fullye have and enjoy his and theire owne judgments and consciences, in matters of religious concernments." But in that same year, even the royal charter to the Anglican proprietors of Carolina recognized freedom of conscience in stipulating that "because it may happen that some of the people and inhabitants of the said province, cannot in their private opinions, conform to the public exercise of religion, according to the liturgy, form and ceremonies of the Church of England . . . and for that the same, by reason of the remote distance of these places, will, we hope be no breach of the unity and uniformity established in this nation [an acknowledgment that the spatial dimension mitigated the necessity of uniform faith and practice]; our will and pleasure therefore is, and we do by these presents, . . . give and grant" the liberty not to follow "for conscience sake" the liturgy and ceremonies, the oaths and articles of the Anglican establishment, provided only that the behavior of religious dissenters not disturb the "peace and safety" or in any way "scandalize . . . the said liturgy, forms and ceremonies." In 1677, the West New Jersey proprietors, in chapter 16 of the *Concessions and Agreements,* asserted that "no men, nor number of men upon earth, hath power or authority to rule over men's consciences in religious matters" and, therefore, that "no person or persons whatsoever within the said province . . . shall . . . upon any pretence whatsoever, be called in question, or in the least punished or hurt, either in person, estate, or privilege, for the sake of his opinion, judgment, faith or worship towards God in matters of religion." In New Hampshire, the Commission of John Cutt to establish a government separate from that of Massachusetts provided that "for the greater ease and satisfaction of our said loving subjects in matters of Religion We do hereby will, require and command that liberty of conscience shall be allowed unto all protestants," and that those who conformed to the rites of the Church of England agree to be "particularly countenanced and encouraged." The New York *Charter of Liberties and Privileges,* adopted in 1683 by the first assembly of deputies to convene in that colony, confirmed the existence of the several Christian churches (Dutch Reformed, Congregational, Presbyterian, and Anglican), established them as "privileged Churches," and guaranteed the same rights to all Christian churches that were to be settled thereafter. In addition, it said that no person professing belief in Christ "shall at any time be any ways molested punished disquieted or called in Question for any Difference in opinion or Matter of Religious Concernment." The New York *Charter of Liberties* was never sustained by the Privy Council, but legislation passed in the 1690's confirmed many of its provisions, including liberty of conscience.

Even Virginia, the province where Anglicanism was first estab-

lished and where it enjoyed the most substantial popular support of any of the Church of England colonies, gave way to the
winds of doctrine sweeping across British America. As early as
1679, a royal instruction to the governor required that, in order
"to give all possible encouragement to persons of different per-
suasions in matters of religion to transport themselves thither
with their stocks, you are not to suffer any man to be molested
or disquieted in the exercise of his religion." Roman Catholics
were subsequently excepted from this imperial directive, which
was later applied to all the royal provinces. Then, in 1699, the
House of Burgesses applied the substance of the Toleration Act
when, in a bill to suppress Sabbath breakers, it exempted dissenters from penalties and forfeitures, provided that they could
prove appropriate attendance at a nonconforming church recognized by the 1689 English statute.

Even in Connecticut, where a religious establishment would
outlast all others save that of Massachusetts, there was a faint
acceptance of religious tolerance as early as 1669, when devi-
ationists from strict orthodoxy who were otherwise sound in
fundamental belief were given "allowance of their persuasion
and profession in church ways or assemblies without disturbance."
Then, in the first decade of the eighteenth century, the entrenched Connecticut establishment granted dissenters the right
to worship in public, provided that they were prepared to continue to give tax support to the Congregational church. In approv-
ing the Saybrook Platform of Church Discipline (1708), a form
of "presbyterial Congregationalism" representing the high point
of Congregational power, the Connecticut Assembly provided
that "nothing herein shall be intended and construed to hinder
or prevent any society or church that is or shall be allowed by
the laws of this government, who soberly differ or dissent from
the united churches hereby established, from exercising worship
and discipline in their own way, according to their consciences"
—a reference to a law passed earlier in the year, which applied
the English Act of Toleration "granting liberties of worshipping
God in a way separate from that which is by law established . . .
without any let, hindrance and molestation whatsoever." Connecticut's little statute of toleration was more an act to appease
the imperial authorities and deflect a move against her by En-

gland than a measured response to local demands for religious liberalism. Even so, it fit the pattern of the times and rounded out the emerging picture of a loosening church establishment.

Thus, from New Hampshire to the Carolinas, the principle of limited religious toleration was adopted to a degree in every English mainland colony by royal instruction, proprietary grant, or provincial enactment. It must be emphasized that liberty of conscience was circumscribed by laws proscribing Quakers, Jews, Unitarians, and Freethinkers, establishing religious tests for office, and depriving particular groups of the right to public worship. Indeed, the condition of American Catholics was probably worse in the eighteenth century than it had been in the seventeenth. Nevertheless, provincial recognition of the principle of toleration, restricted though it was, represented a significant modification of the traditional pattern of church-state relations. Of all the written guarantees of individual freedom that constitutionalists inscribed in the charters and organic laws of the seventeenth-century settlements, "religious toleration was the most frequently encountered provision" (Rutland, 1955:23).

Freedom of conscience in seventeenth-century America was more a response to circumstance than the implementation of any theory of religious liberty. A natural, even logical, solution to the problem of underpopulation, toleration ensured that the newer provinces, particularly those established after the restoration of the Stuart monarchy, would have viability. The refusal to admit openly groups thought to be subversive of fundamental faith—Jews, Quakers, radical Pietists, and Roman Catholics—set limits to the practice of toleration. Still, the breach in the edifice of religious uniformity, once opened, could never be closed. The next century would see the development of the early policy of liberality, narrow though its original parameters may have been.

III

The results of the widespread recognition of freedom of conscience early in our colonial history can best be measured by the dramatic increase in the number, variety, and distribution of churches from the mid-seventeenth to the mid-eighteenth century. The location of the major churches in America in 1650 and 1750, according to the most recent comprehensive tabulation, is shown in Tables I and II.

In 1650, only four colonies (or future colonies) had two or more denominations: Rhode Island, New York, Maryland, and Delaware. All the rest had but one. The Congregational establishment in most of New England and the Anglican establishment of Virginia enjoyed undisputed ecclesiastical hegemony. In Rhode Island and Maryland, the two colonies that openly espoused a policy of toleration, there was already a mixture of churches. Interestingly enough, three of Maryland's four Anglican churches were set up in 1650, one year after the Maryland Toleration Act. What would later be the English colony of New York showed its characteristic religious diversity, with New England's Puritan overflow of Congregationalists and Presbyterians competing with the dominant Dutch Reformed Church. Three of the seven church groups listed (Baptist, Presbyterian, and Roman Catholic) appeared in only one colony, and two others (Anglican and Reformed) in but two. The Lutheran and Congregational churches did have a wider distribution by province, but if we view their placement by general geographic location—that is, in the Middle Atlantic region—instead of within political boundaries, the pattern of regional concentration holds.

By 1750, the picture had changed substantially. Now there was a "mixture" of churches (and synagogues) in every colony, ranging from only three in New Hampshire to seven in South Carolina, New Jersey, and Pennsylvania, and eight in New York. No denomination was found in fewer than five colonies, and two (Presbyterian and Baptist) were found in as many as eleven. Perhaps predictably, the Anglican church had a presence in all of the original Thirteen Colonies. In provinces that, in 1650, had supported a single-church establishment, the pattern of uniformity had been broken; where diversity existed from the start, it intensified. The policy of toleration, widespread by 1700 and even broader by 1750, clearly had the effect of encouraging a proliferation of churches, measured in terms of their over-all distribution and their total number.

TABLE I.

LOCATION OF THE MAJOR CHURCHES IN AMERICA, 1650[a]

Colony	Anglican	Baptist	Congregational	Reformed (Dutch, German and French)	Lutheran	Presbyterian	Roman Catholic	Jewish
New Hampshire (incl. Maine)			3					
Massachusetts			41					
Connecticut			13					
Rhode Island		2	2					
(New York)[b]			1	2	1	4		
(Pennsylvania)[b]					1			
Maryland	4		1				5	
(Delaware)[b]				1	2			
Virginia	26							
Total number in all colonies	30	2	61	3	4	4	5	0
Number of colonies (or future colonies) where found	2	1	6	2	3	1	1	0

TABLE II.

LOCATION OF THE MAJOR CHURCHES IN AMERICA, 1750

Colony	Anglican	Baptist	Congregational	Reformed	Lutheran	Presbyterian	Roman Catholic	Jewish
New Hampshire	1		40			5		
Massachusetts (incl. Maine)	17	16	247			13		
Connecticut	19	12	155		1	1		
Rhode Island	7	30	12					1
New York	20	4	5	59	26	35	1	1
New Jersey	18	14	2	28	19	51	2	
Pennsylvania	19	29		71	73	56	11	1
Maryland	50	4		4	3	18	15	
Delaware	14	2			3	27	1	
Virginia	96	3		5	1	17		
North Carolina	9	13		2	5	9		
South Carolina	16	5	4	6	2	1		1
Georgia	3							1
Total number in all colonies	289	182	465	175	138	233	30	5
Number of colonies where found	13	11	7	7	9	11	5	5

SOURCE: *Ibid.*

IV

The increasing number and variety of churches in the separate colonies strengthened the religious permissiveness that was its initial cause. But other factors deepened the gulf between the old doctrine of a uniform faith within a single-church establishment and the emerging condition of American religious diversity. The whole spirit of the eighteenth century was against coerced belief, organized religious establishments, and even religion itself. On one side, Deism and philosophical rationalism pushed orthodoxy into a defensive posture. Simultaneously, the religious enthusiasm that we associate with the itinerant preachers of the Great Awakening also challenged the *status quo* and the cold and lifeless "Arminianism" of the regular ministry. Beset by these opposite but equally threatening forces, the Protestant churches, which in the sixteenth and seventeenth centuries had divided over fine points of ecclesiology, now faced common enemies: the eighteenth-century Enlightenment and religious fundamentalism. Caught in the middle of this bipolar world, the established churches found that they had more to lose than to gain by alienating dissenting churches that otherwise remained orthodox, in sobriety if not in belief.

Other agents contributed to the breakup of old attitudes governing church-state relations. Commerce, politics, and war were more serious competitors for attention in the eighteenth century than they had been before. The need for population continued, particularly on the frontier, and most colonies preferred to encourage immigrants—often members of left-wing Dissenter or German Pietist groups—to settle in those exposed areas. Still another fact to be reckoned with was plain indifference. Here again, the spatial dimensions of America played a part in changing the position of the church in society. For in addition to moving *away* from one church and *toward* another, many colonists had the additional option of leaving religion and worship altogether. Even after the embers of the Awakening had cooled in coastal regions, the frontier remained alive to religious fundamentalism, because the only preachers available for service in such places were itinerants professing one "enthusiasm" or another. On the frontier, professional clergymen were as rare as lawyers, judges, doctors, and teachers. Moreover, a religious establishment was always a costly legal obligation. Few frontier and breakaway settlements could afford to build a church and keep a minister, even if one were available. And, if the settlers were not homogeneous in faith, several churches would have to be maintained—a capital expenditure far beyond their means. Religious indifference, therefore, was for some a matter not of choice but of circumstance.

Whatever the cause, however, the statistics indicate that the American colonists were among the least "churched" of all Western European peoples. The period from 1650 to 1800 saw a steady decrease in the ratio of churches to total number of inhabitants. In 1650, there were 427 white inhabitants for every church; 631 in 1700; 706 in 1750; and 1,122 in 1800—the highest number of inhabitants per church in our entire history. To put it differently, in 1800 there were fewer churches relative to population than at any other time before or since. Undoubtedly, a major reason for this trend was the economic inability of colonial society to construct churches at a rate commensurate with the dramatic growth of population, but this failure, in turn, contributed to the growth of religious "indifferentism." Although there was regional variation between New England, the Middle Colonies, and the South, the striking fact is the low proportion of population that were regularly affiliated with an organized church, even in places we normally think of as zealously religious. In 1960, over 60 per cent of the American population reported a formal church affiliation, but at the end of the colonial period only 10 per cent were church members.

In the face of such steady attrition, which resulted from physical reality and social conditions as well as from the new currents of thought and feeling, established churches had to seek allies and friends from among erstwhile doctrinal enemies. As a result, the eighteenth-century notion of "denomination" replaced the seventeenth-century notion of "sect." Although the theology behind "denominationalism" has been traced back to a group of Puritan Independents of the period of the English Civil War, the word itself was first used by John Wesley, the founder of

English Methodism. Wesley advanced the idea that the particular names of church groups merely *denominated* their separate existence in the wider body of the Christian Church. Alone, none of them constituted the True Church, but each was merely a variant manifestation of the Church of God. Thus the "denomination" became the basis for a kind of eighteenth-century ecumenicism. This represented a significant shift away from the divisiveness of an earlier period when each splinter group, as it broke off from a parent church, was viewed theologically as false and schismatic.

For a time, the Great Awakening—America's equivalent to England's Methodist upheaval, continental Pietism, and Jewish Hasidism—cultivated the same kind of ecumenical spirit. Thus, for example, in Philadelphia a special house of worship was built by general subscription in order that itinerants of any and every denomination might preach to the awakened populace of that city. Benjamin Franklin, noting the new religiosity that resulted from the visit of the Reverend George Whitefield to Philadelphia in 1739, said that the new building was

> . . . expressly for the Use of any Preacher of any religious Persuasion who might desire to say something to the People of Philadelphia, the Design in building not being to accommodate any particular Sect, but the Inhabitants in general, so that even if the Mufti of Constantinople were to send a Missionary to preach Mahometanism to us, he would find a Pulpit at his Service.

Franklin then indicated that many sects had contributed to the costs of construction, and that "Care was taken in the Nomination of Trustees to avoid giving a Predominancy to any Sect, so that one of each was appointed, *viz.* one Church of England-man, one Presbyterian, one Baptist, one Moravian, etc."

The title deed of the new meeting house authorized the trustees to

> . . . introduce such Protestant ministers to preach the Gospel in the said Houses as they shall judge to be sound in their Principles Zealous and faithful in the Discharge of their Duty and acquainted with the Religion of the Heart and Experimental Piety without any Regard to those Distinctions or differing Sentiments in lesser

matters which have to the scandal of Religion unhappily divided real Christians.

Philadephia's ecumencial response typified the reorientation of the churches, uniting those in every denomination who supported the Great Awakening and dividing them from those who resisted it. Particularly in its early stages, the Awakening cut a broad swathe across the landscape of American Protestantism, separating New Light (and New Side) from Old Light (and Old Side). One historian has gone so far as to suggest that, in the aftermath of the Awakening, only two religious groups remained: those who favored the Awakening and those who opposed it. This is an exaggerated claim. The Awakening's ecumenicism soon dissipated, and its long-term effect was to promote rather than arrest the fragmentation of sects and the proliferation of churches that was already in progress. Still, even this advanced the theme of "denominationalism" and the cause of tolerance. Indeed, in the long run, the Awakening boosted the novel idea that the interests of all the churches of God would be served best if none of them enjoyed a special relationship with the secular state, and if the membership of each were recruited through voluntary association rather than official coercion.

V

All these forces—the proliferation of churches, the rise of "indifferentism," the Great Awakening, and the liberalizing effect of the spreading notion of denominationalism—pushed the doctrine of single-church establishment to its limit until it finally snapped, not all of a sudden but in every province and state, each in its own way. In some places—Virginia, for example—the established church would fall amidst the clatter of a great political struggle; elsewhere, as in Connecticut and Massachusetts, it would slip away more slowly as its irrelevance became ever more evident. Each province—and later each state—would move at its own pace along lines defined by its own religious traditions. The speed and direction of that movement depended partly upon where it began and where it stood in the middle of the eighteenth century.

Richard Hofstadter has summarized the condition of the churches in late colonial America by putting each of the provinces into one of four categories: (1) *old free colonies* with no history of religious establishment—Rhode Island, Pennsylvania, Delaware, and New Jersey; (2) *vacant establishments*, where a single state church did exist but on a very narrow base of popular support—New York, Maryland, the Carolinas, and Georgia; (3) *effective Anglican establishments*—the situation describing Virginia, which alone among the Anglican colonies retained a resemblance to an established church, with substantial, though by no means unchallenged, political and social power; and (4) the *church-state systems* of Massachusetts and Connecticut, a kind of "Puritan imperium" whose influence was felt even beyond the confines of New England. The Puritan establishment was by far the most durable. It survived the Revolution and continued into the nineteenth century, in an attenuated form.

Another and somewhat more illuminating way of analyzing the situation of the churches in late colonial America is to differentiate between *single* and *multiple* establishments. Under the "single establishment with free exercise" (Butts, 1950) arrangement, dissenting bodies are permitted to maintain institutions of public worship, profess unorthodox beliefs, and support ministers and teachers without interference. In some cases this would be in lieu of, in others in addition to, the regular tax for the support of the one established church. Under *multiple establishment,* the state supports all recognized religious institutions equally. This almost amounts to an establishment of religion (as opposed to an establishment of a single church), but it is not quite the same because all religious groups will not receive official recognition and aid. Radical religious communities upholding beliefs thought to be subversive of public order or accepted morals will be either proscribed or deprived of privileges granted to approved bodies. But no single church will be favored over the others. Multiple establishment represents a more advanced step on the road leading away from the traditional, repressive single establishment and toward complete freedom of conscience, but essentially it is still a compromise between the principles of church-state cooperation, at one pole, and absolute religious freedom through church-state separation, at the other.

With these analytical tools, the situation in late colonial America becomes a bit clearer. By the middle of the eighteenth century, all the colonies tolerated the existence of dissenting religious groups, but some went even further by granting state support, either direct or indirect, to more than one church. The trend was unmistakable; it pointed toward liberalization in the form of multiple-church establishment, which had become, by the time of the Revolution, the only politically viable formula for maintaining any kind of church-state relationship.

Thus, New York was, in reality, not a "vacant establishment" but the first and most nearly complete example of multiple establishment. Ever since the Dutch period, New York had supported a welter of religious diversity. When the English took over the province, they continued the policy of toleration that the Dutch West India Company had favored. Under the *Duke's Laws* (1664), any Protestant group with an ordained minister could hold public worship services. Townships were required to support a single church to receive tax support, but the majority of the inhabitants determined the official church, while minority Christian groups were not to be molested in their observances and belief. The *Duke's Laws* did not single out the Church of England for preferential treatment. Despite subsequent efforts by James II and by numerous royal governors to foster an Anglican establishment, the New York Assembly and the settlers themselves consistently resisted efforts to undermine that province's traditional recognition of religious difference. Legislation in 1693 provided that, in the City of New York and in the counties of Richmond, Westchester, and Queens, any "Protestant" minister could satisfy the requirement that each community have a settled minister and church. New York remained committed to the principle of community option in religious affairs, which for all practical purposes resulted in a multiple establishment at the local level.

Even in Massachusetts and Connecticut, multiple establishment was gradually supplanting single establishment before the American Revolution. The Massachusetts Charter of 1691 undermined Congregational dominance by replacing a religious with a property requirement for voting and by mandating liberty of conscience to all Christians except Roman Catholics. But provincial enactments passed in the 1690's preserved the Congregational standing order at the local level for some time. Even in towns where Congregationalists were in the minority, dissenters were unable to overturn the establishment. For example, the General Court in 1715 authorized county courts to step in and force delinquent towns to support the Congregational church, even where the majority of the inhabitants were Quakers. But the Crown opposed such circumventions of the charter. In 1724, it reversed a decision of the General Court authorizing the assessment of several Quaker towns that had failed to provide tax support for the official church. Fear of further Crown interference, plus an increase in the numerical strength of the dissenters and the steady rise of religious indifferentism, strengthened the opponents of the establishment and loosened its control.

In 1727, Massachusetts Anglicans won the right to earmark religious taxes for the support of their own ministers in the so-called Five Mile Act. Any Anglican living within a five-mile radius of his church and in regular attendance could choose to have his church tithe paid to the Anglican minister. Baptists and Quakers won similar privileges the following year. Neither group, however, was satisfied with such limited concessions. Both rejected the proposition that their adherents should be forced, through the taxing power of the state, into giving financial support to ministers and churches—even their own. While the Act of 1728 exempted Quakers and Baptists from a poll tax for the upkeep of religion, it did not exempt their properties and estates from taxation and they continued to be required to pay their full share for the upkeep of orthodox church buildings. In addition, Quakers and Baptists objected to the five-mile stipulation, as well as several other onerous requirements in the legislation. In the years that followed, both groups forced a number of concessions from the General Court. By 1734, Quaker and Baptist estates were exempt from tax; their exemption included church upkeep; and the five-mile law was rescinded—a privilege that the legislature extended to Anglicans a year later.

To be sure, dissenting churches, after 1735, continued to face serious practical and legal disabilities that kept them in an inferior position relative to the Congregational establishment. Towns resisted the granting of tax relief because this increased tax burdens for orthodox-church members. In fact, if a drop in revenues resulting from a high number of exemptions forced a reduction in the minister's salary, a town could pass a supplementary assessment that could be imposed on Anglicans (though not on Quakers or Baptists). Other annoyances persisted. The expense and difficulty of obtaining certificates of exemption were always burdensome. After the Great Awakening, when Separates —those who broke with the old-line Congregational churches—became Baptists in order to take advantage of their exemption from all religious assessments, the General Court attempted to tighten up the tax-relief laws, and the recently converted were subjected to legal harassment. Later on, newly appointed dissenting ministers had to be approved by a board of county ministers—usually Congregationalists—before they could be "settled." In addition, dissenters in new towns were forced to support the establishment until the town was officially incorporated, a procedure that often took several years. Finally, Anglicans who lived too far from their churches to comply with the law requiring regular attendance were ineligible for tax relief.

Thus, by the end of the colonial period, Massachusetts stood somewhere between single and multiple establishment. The law still favored Congregationalism, but the dissenting churches had made significant inroads into Congregational hegemony. The Revolution would see the completion of the transition to multiple establishment. When the Massachusetts Constitution of 1780 allowed that "all monies paid by the subject to the support of public worship . . . shall, if he require it, be uniformly applied to the support of the public teacher or teachers of his own religious sect or denomination" (Article III), it extended and gave constitutional sanction to a policy that had been in the process of development for over half a century.

There is evidence that, in practice, Connecticut allowed Anglican dissenters from the Congregational church to earmark their taxes for the support of their own ministers, even before the right was recognized in law. Connecticut's act for the relief of

dissenters, passed in 1727, was the legislature's positive response
to a protest against an attempt by the town of Fairfield to force
Anglicans to abide by legal regulations that they had apparently
been flouting for some time. Two years later, exemption privileges were extended to Quakers and Baptists—the other major
dissenting groups in Connecticut.

In a number of ways, the relief and exemption laws passed in
Connecticut in the late 1720's were more liberal than the Massachusetts enactments. There was no five-mile limit in the Connecticut statutes, although court decisions did impose a two-mile
limit for a time. Connecticut did not have the special obligation
that Massachusetts Anglicans had of paying for supplemental
appropriations to maintain the salaries of Congregational ministers threatened by reductions resulting from dissenter exemptions. In addition, estates as well as polls were exempt from tax
from the very beginning, and the exemptions included church
buildings as well as minister maintenance. Finally, exemption
certificates did not have to be renewed each year in Connecticut:
the exemption acts themselves were permanent. In Massachusetts, periodic renewal put dissenter freedoms in a chronic state
of insecurity.

As in Massachusetts, the Congregational churches in Connecticut continued to enjoy special status. The requirement that
dissenters obtain certificates was humiliating, and many were
undoubtedly discouraged from applying for it. Moreover, dissenters claiming a tax exemption in Connecticut had to be members
of their respective churches, not merely regular attendants.
Viewed in its entirety, however, the liberalization of the late
1720's significantly broadened the base of the religious establishment in Connecticut. As Sanford H. Cobb, the historian of
American religious liberty, put it: The Connecticut legislation of
the 1720's "incorporated the dissenting Churches into the Church
establishment" (1902:269–70).

Even when, as a result of the disturbances occasioned by the
Great Awakening, a temporary stiffening of the establishment's
posture caused the enactment of restrictions regarding the incorporation of new churches, this legislation merely imposed on
dissenters the same requirements governing new Congregational

churches. The conservative reaction to the Great Awakening, which was nowhere more pronounced than in Connecticut, could not arrest the erosion of the standing order. Starting in 1750, with the New Light Separates of Milford, and ending in 1777, when all Separates were released from the obligation to support Old Light churches, religious dissension within the establishment itself achieved formal recognition. Thus, by the end of the colonial period, the combined efforts of Anglicans, traditional dissenters, and Separates in Connecticut "had helped to undermine the foundation of the established church" (Zeichner, 1949:101).

New Hampshire was the last of the group of provinces in which multiple establishment was either achieved or in the process of completion by the late colonial period. With the exception of New York, New Hampshire was probably the first to experiment with an alternative to a province-wide religious establishment. In both colonies, the minister was selected and supported by the local inhabitants. The law of 1693 setting up a church establishment allowed for conscientious exemption; that is, dissenters could be granted relief from church taxes if they could prove to the satisfaction of local authorities that they were supporting some other church. Because there were few, if any, such churches in being in the late seventeenth and early eighteenth centuries, however, this exemption proved to be a dead letter; a *de facto* single establishment came into being despite the liberal allowances of the law.

The eighteenth century witnessed the struggle of dissenter groups to obtain in practice what this legal regime permitted in theory. The burden of proof, however, rested on the claimant for exemption, and local selectmen withheld concessions to dissenters less on doctrinal grounds than because of their reluctance to give up needed tax revenues. Exemptions always meant higher levies for the orthodox. Moreover, unlike dissenters in Massachusetts, Connecticut, and New York, in most cases dissenting churches in New Hampshire could not utilize the town authorities to collect their revenues for them. Except for some New Hampshire Presbyterian congregations, once exemptions had been granted the churches were completely dependent upon the voluntary support of their parishioners. In that sense, therefore, the elements of multiple establishment in New Hampshire were somewhat weaker than in other provinces, since the dominant Congregational church alone enjoyed the benefit of official support in the collection of revenues.

Still, New Hampshire was probably the most liberal of the orthodox Puritan colonies. The principle of exemption from compulsory taxation for reasons of conscience was recognized in New Hampshire in 1693, a generation before the exemption laws of Massachusetts and Connecticut. William G. McLoughlin, a leading historian of early New England dissent, has called this a "landmark in the history of religious liberty in New England. It set a precedent for toleration in New Hampshire which, despite numerous infractions of its spirit, made that province the freest of the Puritan colonies before the development of Vermont" (1971: II, 836–37).

In fact, it is difficult to generalize about the character of the religious establishment in provincial New Hampshire because the situation varied so greatly from town to town. Some towns had single establishments with virtually no free exercise, others had dual or multiple establishments, and some had no established church whatsoever. The local strength of the Congregationalists usually determined the viability of other groups. Nevertheless, by the eve of the Revolution it was clear that New Hampshire did not support a single province-wide church establishment. Quakers, Anglicans, Presbyterians, and Baptists had achieved equal recognition and acceptance. The right of New Light Congregationalists not to support old-line orthodox churches was acknowledged earlier than in Connecticut and Massachusetts. By the end of the colonial period, New Hampshire had become, in fact as well as in law, a member of the multiple-establishment camp.

VI

Thus, in New York, Massachusetts, Connecticut, and New Hampshire, wherever the law left the choice of minister to the individual towns or allowed tax revenues to be assigned to more than one religious group, some form of multiple establishment was in existence before the end of the colonial period. As Leonard Levy has written, "The pattern of establishment was diversified and uniquely American" (1972:192). According to the Hofstadter formulation, the New England establishment was the strongest and most vital kind of church-state relation in existence in America in the late colonial period. Measured by durability, there is some truth in this statement. The fact that Massachusetts, Connecticut, and New Hampshire were to be the last of the original Thirteen Colonies to relinquish a religious establishment supports this judgment. But a major reason that some kind of church establishment survived the disestablishmentarian impulses of the Revolution was that in New England the orthodox and the dissenter had worked out a special kind of compromise and accommodation. Indeed, it was precisely because of its flexibility on these issues that New England Puritanism—which we normally identify with hidebound rigidity on such matters—managed to maintain a semblance of the traditional alliance between church and state in the early national period. Elsewhere, attempts to adhere to more rigorous forms of church establishment resulted in complete collapse.

The best example of this failure is Virginia, the strongest of the single-establishment colonies, but by the 1750's already embroiled in a crisis of authority that would bring, in the course of the Revolution, first disestablishment and then a paradigmatic separation of religion and the state. The Clergy Act of October, 1748, which, among other things, gave the Anglican pastors greater security of tenure than they had ever enjoyed, represented the high point of the church's power in Virginia. From then to the Revolution, the road was downhill, as internal structural weaknesses, social discontents, anticlericalism, and dissenter pressures broke through the surface calm of the standing order. In the generation preceding 1776, settlement beyond the Blue Ridge intensified, and a large number of immigrants—Scotch-Irish Presbyterians for the most part—moved into the western counties. Since 1720, Virginia had temporarily exempted some dissenter groups from having to support the Anglican churches that, by law, needed to be built and maintained in every district. Although this, in itself, did not represent a direct threat to the single establishment, the social consequences of encouraging the settlement of dissident elements were soon apparent. In the western regions, Anglicans were a clear minority, while Presbyterians dominated the vestries, the principal organ of clerical and civic authority at the local level of government. Ministerial salaries, fixed by local regulations controlling the rate of exchange for tobacco, were kept low. In one parish, the Presbyterian vestry attempted to satisfy the requirement of having a regular church by forcing the Anglicans to hold services in the county court house. Everywhere, church establishments were a heavy public burden, but in frontier areas, where none had existed and where the majority were not of an Anglican affiliation, it must have seemed altogether absurd to create and support religious institutions merely to satisfy statutory requirements that had little relevance to local needs and wishes.

But even in the settled eastern portions of the province, Anglicanism was in trouble. The clergy itself did not enjoy the position and independence that men of authority were expected to have in Virginia society. Thus, until about 1750, a great number of the Virginia ministry, though English-born, came from a somewhat lower social station than the typical English pastor at home. In addition, in all of the Anglican parishes, central authority was weak at best. In contrast to the situation in England, Church of England parishes in Virginia were highly independent, probably even more so than the independent churches of Congregational New England. These facts, plus the chronic attacks of the Awakeners on the Virginia clergy for alleged immorality and degeneracy, fostered a widespread anticlericalism among the Virginia gentry that led, after 1740, to an exodus from establishment to dissent. Continuing defections of the common people to New Light Presbyterianism in the Awakening of the 1740's and early 1750's further exacerbated the crisis of the Anglican Church.

Other forces helped to weaken the Anglican grip on provincial Virginia. Enemy pressure on the frontier during the French and Indian War reduced resistance to dissenter demands that their preachers be allowed to move and work more freely about the colony. The rise of the more radical Separate Baptists and the Methodists, in the 1760's, made traditional dissenters such as the Presbyterians seem more staid and acceptable. Finally, the Parsons' Cause, which pitted clerical interests against the Virginia Assembly and brought about a constitutional struggle between the colony and England, intensified the crisis of confidence in the Virginia establishment in this same period. Undoubtedly, the troubles that beset the Anglican church in Virginia were part of the deep social crisis that helped to generate the Revolution; as the most recent student of the subject has put it, "The difficulties of the Church revealed the weakest link in the chain of traditional authority at a point where popular pressures were most acutely felt" (Isaac, 1973:36). But, viewed from within the more limited parameters of church history and from the perspective of what was happening in the other single-establishment colonies—Maryland, Georgia, and the Carolinas—the problems of the Virginia establishment were simply the most acute manifestation of the disintegration of the traditional pattern of church-state relations which colonial conditions had at last revealed.

VII

The American Revolution had the effect of shifting those colonies with a single predominant church to multiple establishment or, where multiple establishment was still only partial, of bringing it to completion. Where multiple establishment was fully mature, however, the Revolution pushed the more advanced notion of complete disestablishment, nurtured by the emerging theory of church-state separation, to the forefront of public policy.

Recent discussions of the meaning of the First Amendment to the federal Constitution have questioned the degree to which the principle of separation of church and state was accepted in the period immediately after the Revolution. A growing body of literature critical of the Supreme Court's use of history—most notably in *Everson* v. *Board of Education* (1947)—has challenged the liberal interpretation of the Amendment's religious clauses on several grounds: First, the Virginia Statute of Religious Freedom (1786) was a *unique* example of an *extreme* position, and

Jefferson's "wall of separation" was "eccentric" and not reflective of the consensus of opinion in the states in the early national period. Second, the very vagueness of the establishment clause— "Congress shall make no law *respecting an establishment of religion*"—was designed to prevent any tampering with the religious establishments that still prevailed in New England and, in particular, to bar Congress or the federal courts from undermining contractual obligations between ministers and churches there. Third, Americans were dedicated to the establishment of a Protestant Christian nation, and religious liberty was tolerable only so long as it did not jeopardize that commitment. Fourth, the nonestablishment clause of the First Amendment was meant not to protect disbelief but to maintain the "sympathetic neutrality" of the government among competing religious groups. Fifth, organized religious institutions could not survive without state aid, either through tax support of one kind or another or through legal incorporation, which enabled churches to sue parishioners for unpaid assessments. Even the more radical denominations like the Baptists began to forswear absolutist notions of church-state separation as they recognized their dependence upon the machinery of the law. The result was a new kind of *"de facto* establishment" (Howe, 1965:15), a "symbiotic relationship between church and state" (McLoughlin, 1973:249), which has continued to the present time.

There are a number of problems with this narrow, revisionist view of the First Amendment. To begin with, it takes no account of the fact that, in 1800, there were fewer people affiliated with organized churches than at any other time in our history. What were the consequences of this striking statistic in terms of the changing ideology of church-state relations? Could it not reasonably be argued that the great mass of the population, nominally Protestant to be sure, was tired of church-related issues, was no longer prepared to support churches as public institutions and was quite sympathetic to the Jeffersonian argument of the impropriety of any bond between church and state in a republican society? On the question of "accommodations" between religion and the state, such as the right of legal incorporation, what, after all, do such accommodations prove? Separation of church and state does not mean that the law takes no cognizance of religious bodies. The law impinges upon and shapes the most private and intimate of human concerns, and it is no surprise that this has happened in the realm of religion. Even James Madison, author of the Virginia *Memorial and Remonstrance* (1785), which paved the way for the Statute of Religious Freedom, and the man who, as President, applied the principle of separation, recognized this. Writing to the president of Charleston College in 1832, he said:

> I must admit moreover that it may not be easy, in every possible case, to trace the line of separation between the rights of religion and the Civil authority with such distinctness as to avoid collisions & doubts on unessential points. The tendency to a usurpation on one side or the other, or to a corrupting coalition or alliance between them, will be best guarded against by an entire abstinence of the Government from interference in any way whatever, beyond the necessity of preserving public order, & protecting each sect against trespasses on its legal rights by others.

Or, as Justice Frankfurter said, in dissent, in the second Flag Salute Case (*West Virginia State Board of Education* v. *Barnette* [1943]):

> Religion is outside the sphere of political government. This does not mean that all matters on which religious organizations or beliefs may pronounce are outside the sphere of government. Were this so, instead of the separation of church and state, there would be the subordination of the state on any matter deemed within the sovereignty of the religious conscience. Much that is the concern of temporal authority affects the spiritual interests of men.

The fundamental conceptual weakness of the revisionists is that they fail to comprehend the perfect compatibility of strict separation with a fully religious society. There was, after all, no man more dedicated to spiritual purity and the integrity of religious institutions than Roger Williams, but, as the revisionists have pointed out, it was Williams who first conceived the "wall of separation" metaphor. The purpose of the First Amendment, and of the parallel provisions of early state constitutions and statutes where disestablishment occurred, was to achieve a secular state and not a secularized society. The revisionists have confused the two. It would be unrealistic to suppose that the generation that decided to fashion a secular state knew precisely what its implications or its public-policy imperatives were. The ramifications of separation were not known in advance. Nor is it surprising that old practices persisted in the states and on the federal level even after disestablishment and the adoption of the First Amendment: The use of chaplains in legislative assemblies as well as in Congress, land grants to churches and church-related activities, proclamations of fast days and the other promotional acts of government continued as a result of a cultural momentum built up in the past. The word "establishment" itself continued to have a very restricted meaning in the early republic. Thus, in upholding a conviction for blasphemy, Chief Justice James Kent of New York could say, "Though the constitution has discarded religious establishments, it does not forbid judicial cognizance of those offenses against religion and morality which have no references to any such establishment." (*People* v. *Ruggles* [1811]). Baptists had no difficulty with proclamations of days of prayer and thanksgiving or with public grants of land to churches, even though they had consistently championed the principle of separation.

The separation of church from state has been a gradual process. The First Amendment was a landmark on a long road reaching back into the colonial past. Its adoption did not signify full realization of the consequences of that principle, but it was a response to the felt impulses of the time. It was a product of the new ideology of republicanism that the Revolution had fathered. It must be remembered that the big issue at the time of the Framing was multiple establishment, which was resoundingly defeated everywhere except in New England, where its demise was only more protracted. No state created after the Founding of the Republic established either a single church or religion in general. The defeat of the "general assessment" plan in Virginia is well known. Those states that considered or actually experimented with a religious establishment either for Christians in general or for Protestants only—

Maryland, South Carolina, and Georgia—found it unworkable and soon abandoned the idea. Where multiple establishment on a nonpreferential basis was longstanding, the Revolution forced a more complete disestablishment and separation of church and state. And where no regular religious establishment had ever existed—New Jersey, Pennsylvania, Delaware, Rhode Island—the Revolution merely affirmed prior experience. Except for Rhode Island, which continued under its colonial charter, all these states adopted new constitutions barring compulsory support for religious institutions. Finally, the most convincing interpretation of the cloudy legislative history of the religious clauses of what became the First Amendment shows that the Framers intended to prohibit Congress from sanctioning a multiple rather than just a single establishment (Levy, 1972:179–187).

Thus, the American Revolution did not bring about sweeping changes of a uniform character in church-state relations. Rather, it accelerated tendencies already in motion in the colonial period, legitimated departures from the traditional model of a single church establishment, and broadened support for the still radical idea of complete separation of church and state.

VIII

In America, the notion that church and state ought to remain in distinct spheres and that any mixing of the two would corrupt each started with Roger Williams, but for the rest of the seventeenth century, what one commentator has called the "idiom" of establishment dominated public life. William Penn—with Williams, the other great American apostle of religious freedom—stood for broad toleration, as a tenet of his Quaker faith, rather than for strict separation. Pennsylvania was, after all, a "holy experiment" in civil government. Not until the eighteenth century did the echoes of Roger Williams begin to reverberate with any regularity. By 1750, they were not only clearly audible but widespread.

Lawrence Leder has uncovered a number of examples of professions of the separation doctrine in this period. As early as 1712, one Thomas Maule lamented the "woeful consequence of this hodge podge mess of medley, and jumbling of church and state together again." Some years later, a South Carolina Presbyterian, the Reverend Josiah Smith, observed that the Reformation was justified by the principle of separation, which alone distinguished Protestantism from Roman Catholicism. In New England, too, there was an observable growth of an intellectual challenge to traditional views. In 1739, the Reverend Charles Chauncy, pastor of Boston's First Church and a leading religious conservative, suggested that the state had no place in the enforcement of belief. "[T]he use of force in matters of religion and conscience," he said, "is not only contrary to the example of Christ . . . but to the nature and reason of things."

For the most part, such professions of religious liberty were confined to dissenters from prevailing orthodoxies or to those speaking out of the nonconformist tradition. Moreover, men like the rationalist Jonathan Mayhew, who argued for private judgment and freedom from secular coercion in religious matters, did not mean that the church ought to be completely divorced from the secular state. Advocacy of "freedom of conscience" was, in fact, perfectly compatible with multiple establishment, which was beginning to emerge as social reality in New England at this time. But there is surely a relationship—even a progression—from one idea to the other. "Matters of religion relate to another world and have nothing to do with the interest of the state," the Presbyterian William Livingston said in 1753, in denouncing the projected establishment of an Anglican college in New York. Livingston was arguing against what he took to be an element of incipient establishment, but in his language was the seed for the philosophical growth of the separation idea. One bordered on and led to the other, particularly in places, like New York, where circumstances were stretching traditional doctrines to the breaking point.

In 1768, on the eve of the Revolution, John Dickinson of Pennsylvania wrote:

> Religion and government are certainly very different Things, instituted for different Ends; the Design of one being to promote our temporal Happiness; the Design of the other to procure the

Favor of G-d, and thereby the Salvation of our Souls. While these are kept distinct and apart, the Peace and Welfare of Society is preserved, and the Ends of both answered. But by mixing them together, Feuds, Animosities and Persecutions have been raised, which have deluged the World in Blood, and disgraced human Nature.

The clarity of Dickinson's formulation suggests that it marks a maturation of a concept that was to achieve institutional reinforcement and increased popular acceptance in the coming decades. Standing between Roger Williams and John Dickinson was the colonial history of America, the growth of toleration, the recognition of a right to conscience, the emerging ideology of religious equality, and the social and intellectual cross-currents of the eighteenth century. By the end of the colonial era, American society supported multiform patterns of church-state relations, but the course of development was well set. Multiple establishment would prove to be but a temporary and unsteady compromise between traditional models of church-state relations and genuine spiritual freedom. By the time of the First Amendment, the whole idea of a religious establishment was giving way under pressures that had been building up for a very long time. By the time of the Revolution, separation of church and state was not the normative standard defining the relationship between church and state; but to the extent that religious conditions in colonial society pointed in that direction—and an emerging ideology of separation reinforced that tendency—it can be claimed as a product of the colonial experience.

5

The Condition of the Press

Historians have been telling us for some years now that government instrumentalities of one kind or another severely restricted the freedom of the press in colonial America. Royal governors acting under the authority of their instructions continued to issue licenses to printers, thereby exercising some control over newspapers, until about 1730—a generation after prior censorship died in England, with the expiration of the Licensing Act, in 1695. In the seventeenth century, and to some extent in the early eighteenth, laws against blasphemy and heresy were available for use to punish anticlerical or antireligious publications; but increasingly, in the new secular age, the more common offenses to the established order were criticisms of the state rather than of the church. Libel and sedition replaced blasphemy and heresy as the major offenses that invited repression. At first, the court trial was the most likely forum in which the government could proceed against troublesome authors, editors, and printers. Then, in the middle decades of the eighteenth century, the scene shifted from the courtroom to the assembly hall. Colonial legislatures became the major menace to a free press. The threat—and often the reality—of legislative process rather than judicial trial against individuals had, it is said, a stifling effect upon the development of press freedom.

The pivotal episode in the story of colonial journalism was

the celebrated case of John Peter Zenger, whose trial and acquittal in 1735 has been looked upon for generations as the real
beginning of a free press in America. As every schoolchild knows,
Zenger was originally from Germany. With his family, he had
emigrated to America as a boy. His mother apprenticed him to
William Bradford, New York's public printer and the founder
of one of the great colonial printing families. In 1726, Zenger
went into business for himself. His *Weekly Journal* began publication in 1733, as the political organ of the most powerful
opposition faction to the governor of the colony, William Cosby.
From the fall of 1733 until Zenger's arrest, the *Journal* was involved in a hot "paper war" against the Cosby regime. Zenger
published the libertarian essays of Thomas Gordon and John
Trenchard, personal attacks upon the governor himself, and fake
advertisements ridiculing the governor's associates; on the other
side, Bradford's *New-York Gazette* defended the regime. Governor Cosby was determined to suppress public criticism and
felt impelled to move. In November, 1734, he had Zenger arrested for seditious libel.

When Zenger's two attorneys, James Alexander and William
Smith, were disbarred for calling into question the commissions
of the two Supreme Court justices before whom the case was to
be tried, Zenger's supporters managed to recruit Andrew Hamilton of Philadelphia, reputed to be the best trial lawyer in the
colonies. Hamilton's defense rested on bad law, but his argument
won an acquittal from the jury. He reasoned that, in seditious-
libel cases, the jury should have the right to decide not only
whether the accused had published the material in question but
whether that material was true or false. The accepted legal
doctrine was that writings or publications that defamed a public
official and had the effect of provoking hatred, contempt, or
ridicule breached the public peace, whether they were true or
not. The provocation and not its truth or falsehood was the
offense that was subject to criminal penalty. According to the
prevailing view, this in no way impaired the freedom of the press,
which consisted, as Blackstone would later put it, "in laying no
previous restraints upon publications, and not in freedom from
censure for criminal matters when published" (*Commentaries,*

IV, 151). In contrast, Hamilton argued that truth was a defense in a prosecution for seditious libel and that only false criticism of the government was punishable. Freedom of the press meant, among other things, freedom to criticize injustice. This was the best protection for popular liberties and constitutional government. Hamilton canonized the role of the jury who, as guardians of liberty, had to review not merely the fact of publication but its content as well. Thus, his position was more of a constitutional argument than a strictly legal defense of Zenger. The law was clearly on the government's side.

Although Zenger was acquitted on the strength of Hamilton's impassioned appeal to constitutional liberty and the obligations of juries, the Zenger case had little immediate effect on the common law of seditious libel either in England or in the American colonies. Legal doctrine did not change in this field for more than half a century. At best, the Zenger case showed that juries were an unreliable support for prosecutions by unpopular colonial governors. As a result, court trials of seditious-libel cases soon diminished, not only because of the reluctance of petit jurors to convict but also because grand jurors refused to indict.

But if judges acting under royal commissions were no longer the chief inquisitors of printers and editors, houses of assembly and governors' councils quickly filled the void. The major cases occurring between Zenger in 1735 and the outbreak of the Revolution all involved actions brought by legislative bodies on grounds of either libel or breach of legislative privilege. In 1742, the Massachusetts Council brought an action against Thomas Fleet of the *Boston Evening Post* for libeling the administration of Sir Robert Walpole. At about this time, William Parks, publisher of the *Virginia Gazette,* was accused by the Virginia House of Burgesses of libeling one of its members. In 1753, Hugh Gaine of the *New-York Mercury* was summoned to the Assembly to explain why he had presumed to publish its proceedings without leave. Three years later, James Parker, Gaine's competitor, was jailed for one week by order of the House for reporting distress among the people of Orange and Ulster counties, which the legislature interpreted as a bad reflection on itself. Between 1756 and 1758, William Smith, provost of the College of Philadelphia, was called to the bar and twice jailed for his printed criticisms of the Assembly, which were considered a breach of privilege. In 1770, Alexander McDougall was jailed for publishing a broadside attacking the legislature for voting supplies to provision the local English garrison. Released when the government's principal witness, James Parker, died, McDougall was summoned for examination by the House. When he refused to respond to interrogation, a vote was taken and he was recommitted to confinement. In 1773, the governor's council in South Carolina summoned Thomas Powell, printer of the *South Carolina Gazette,* to appear before it for publishing a protest authored by William Drayton and William Henry Drayton, two dissenting councilmen who were later to become leading South Carolina patriots. Powell was charged with contempt and breach of privilege. He was released at the trial of his habeas corpus petition on the ground that the council was not a true legislative body but more in the nature of a privy council and therefore without the punitive powers it claimed. In short, as Leonard W. Levy (1966:xxxvi), has argued:

> The Zenger case at best gave the press the freedom to print the "truth"—if the truth were not directed against the legislature. The power of the legislature to punish nonmembers as well as members for alleged breach of privilege—criticism of the assembly— enabled it to control the press.

From this analysis a rather bleak picture of the condition of the colonial press emerges. Daniel Boorstin (1958:333), describing the "conservative" press of the era, says that, in Philadelphia, "libel trials and suppression of the opposition press were common . . . until the eve of the Revolution." He conveys the impression of a press that was the handmaiden of government, lackluster in content, and devoid of vigor. From his extensive work in the field, Leonard Levy (1960) concluded:

> The persistent image of colonial America as a society which cherished freedom of expression is a sentimental hallucination that ignores history. . . . In colonial America, as in England, the common law of seditious libel was strung out like a chicken wire of

constraint making the open discussion of public issues hazardous, if not impossible, except when public opinion opposed administration policy.

One wonders, however, whether the case has not been overstated, and whether historians have not gone beyond their evidence in arriving at such dismal conclusions. Granted that the common law of seditious libel continued to be good law down to the end of the century, that the Zenger case had little immediate impact upon legal doctrine, and that legislatures used their newly won independence and power to suppress offensive material—does this mean that a vigorous press was absent from American life in the late colonial period? The answer must be that, on the basis of the kind of evidence recent writers have uncovered, we cannot tell. We have learned much about attitudes toward freedom of the press and the legal parameters of press freedom in the eighteenth century, but we need to know more about the actual condition of the press during this period of judicial and legislative restriction. For example, the emphasis on the law of seditious libel has obscured the real importance of Zenger's *Journal* as opposed to Zenger's trial. Unlike most newspapers of the period, the *Weekly Journal* was avowedly political. Politics was its reason for being; all else was secondary. In this respect, it was a major journalistic innovation, the real foundation of the tradition of political journalism in America. If Zenger's case really did not matter, the *New York Weekly Journal* certainly did.

The concentrated attention to examples of legislative suppression and the ferreting out of every last case of supposed intimidation distort the image. The mere citation of cases does not make it clear whether they were the rule or the exception. In those cases where editors or printers were condemned to jail or fined for costs, the sentences were short and the penalties minimal. The victims were amply compensated by increased notoriety, which may very well have enhanced circulation. We assume that legal restrictions on press freedom, the ever present threat of official reprisals, and occasional exemplary prosecutions by the courts or the legislature were intimidating; but these may very well have been the acceptable risks of the printing trade. Zenger, for example, does not appear to have been humbled by his incarceration from November, 1734, until his release in August, 1735. The *Weekly Journal* continued its vituperative attacks upon the Cosby regime during his absence under James Alexander's uninterrupted editorial management. Zenger emerged from jail a popular hero. Subsequently, when a new regime came to power, he was appointed public printer for the colony.

II

More important than government restriction, intimidation, and outright suppression in limiting the press were the sheer physical and technical difficulties of gathering, publishing, and distributing news, the financial risks of printing as a business enterprise, and the professional traditions, attitudes, and practices that governed eighteenth-century journalism. Most of the essential materials of production—newsprint, ink, presses, and type—had to be imported from abroad at considerable expense. No type foundry existed in the American colonies until 1768; the only type available for export out of Britain was secondhand. The first printing press was not manufactured domestically until 1769. Printer's ink was not made in quantity until after the Revolution, although local printers sometimes produced their own at great inconvenience. Paper was milled in America, but it was of a cheaper quality than the imported commodity. Benjamin Franklin, the most successful printer in America, derived part of his income at the height of his career from manufacturing and selling ink and newsprint to printers in other colonies with whom he was in partnership.

In the early days of colonial journalism, local news was not considered important enough to warrant space in a local paper. In small communities, everyone knew what happened without having to read about it in the press. "News" meant foreign news —the latest happenings from abroad—except that the time span separating the event itself and the published report of it was often many months, so that colonial newspapers were often chronicles of recent history rather than journals of current events.

In winter, when bad weather delayed ships or postriders, editors often printed trivia. Successful newspaper printers usually had to keep in touch with regular "correspondents," who forwarded news by letter from the principal towns along the seaboard or even from abroad.

One of the tendencies of eighteenth-century American journalism, however, was a gradually decreased interest in foreign news in favor of local and intercolonial news. As population grew and social and political affairs became more complex and difficult to understand firsthand, readers began to expect more local reportage, interpretation, and commentary. After extensive analysis of the colonial press, Richard L. Merritt concludes that, before 1738, only one-fourth of a cross-section of colonial papers published "original"—that is, colonial—news as opposed to foreign news, but thereafter there was a marked increase in local and intercolonial material and a relative decline in the attention devoted to news from abroad. But as newspapers began striking closer to home, printers faced the increasingly difficult problem of deciding what local news to include and what to leave out.

Most newspaper publishers were businessmen primarily—printers first and journalists second. What they printed was not so important as keeping the presses going. As a result, newspaper printers were often highly mercurial in their politics. Hugh Gaine, for example, oscillated throughout his career between one side of important public questions and the other. On the debate over the founding of King's College in New York, in the early 1750's, Gaine at first adamantly refused to print the works of the Presbyterian opponents of the Anglican establishment, but later his paper was so filled with anti-Anglican material that he appears to have switched his position. During the Revolution, Gaine began as a printer for the patriot cause; but, when things went badly for the Whigs in New York, he went to work for the British when they occupied the city. Gaine was more unpredictable than most, but his attitude was not in conflict with the prevailing ethical standards of the printing profession. Those standards comported well with business necessity.

The newspaper was only an adjunct to the printer's other business activities. The average printer imported and retailed a wide assortment of goods—not only books of all kinds (almanacs, grammars, Bibles, law books, dictionaries, novels, and scientific treatises) but also household remedies, hardware, musical instruments, wax, leather goods, paper, and firearms. His newspaper was his principal means of self-advertisement. A main source of income was job printing—turning out specialty items in lots for private firms, churches, and sundry organizations. For Philadelphia printers, it was the "first order of business" (Parker, 1966:27).

The newspapers did not, in themselves, make money, but they did keep the printer's name before the public, thus maintaining the flow of orders for specialty work as well as advertising the arrival of his most recent shipment of goods from abroad. That is why delinquent subscribers, sometimes several years in arrears, continued to receive their journals. James Parker, public printer for New York, estimated, in 1759, that at least 25 per cent of his subscribers were normally behind in their subscription payments. The printer had to keep his name and his advertising in circulation. But this dependence on subscriptions tended to dictate the content of what was published. It meant, for one thing, that a printer could not exclude letters or essays with which he disagreed. A "free press" meant an open press. Benjamin Franklin summed up this credo of the trade in his "Apology for Printers" (1731):

> Printers are educated in the Belief, that when Men differ in Opinion, both Sides ought equally to have the Advantage of being heard by the Publick; and that when Truth and Error have fair Play, the former is always an overmatch for the latter: Hence they chearfully serve all contending Writers that pay them well, without regarding on which side they are of the Question in Dispute. Being thus continually employ'd in serving both Parties, Printers naturally acquire a vast Unconcernedness as to the right or wrong Opinions contained in what they print; regarding it only as the Matter of their daily labour. . . . That it is unreasonable to imagine Printers approve of every thing they print, and to censure them on any particular thing accordingly; since in the way of their Business they print such great variety of things opposite and contradictory. It is likewise as unreasonable what some assert, "That

Printers ought not to print any Thing but what they approve";
since if all of that Business should make such a Resolution, and
abide by it, an End would thereby be put to Free Writing, and the
World would afterwards have nothing to read but what happen'd
to be the Opinions of Printers. That if all Printers were determin'd
not to print any thing till they were sure it would offend no body,
there would be very little printed.

During the press war over Kings' College, in 1753, Hugh Gaine
was assailed for preventing the "triumvirate"—William Livingston, William Smith, Jr., and John Morin Scott—from replying
to attacks on their *Independent Reflector* that appeared in Gaine's
New-York Mercury. Gaine was accused, in effect, of restricting
the press. Most printers, however, followed Franklin's philosophy
(or business methods) and tried to keep their pages open to
opposing viewpoints. This broadened their appeal and sustained
interest in the journal's weekly reappearance.

The average printer might avoid publishing controversial
material if the effect would be to terminate subscriptions. The
best illustration of this was, again, the storm raging around the
Independent Reflector. James Parker published both the *New
York Gazette* and the *Reflector*. When twelve subscribers dropped
their orders for the *Gazette* after Parker had reprinted material
from the early issues of the magazine, he immediately announced
a change in policy and refused thereafter to allow the pages
of his weekly to be used by the editors of his own monthly.
Eventually, he discontinued the *Reflector* altogether. The Parker
case is but one example of a general truism about newspaper
journalism: Newspapers reflect the attitudes of their readership
as much as, if not more than, they affect them. The very nature
of the colonial printer's enterprise and the practices of most
newspaper publishers in the colonial period probably had more
to do with defining the character of the press than repressive
legal doctrines of press freedom and government intimidation.

III

Given the obstacles to the development of journalism in the
colonies—the narrowness of the law, the physical hardships of
transporting papers from place to place over long distances, the

difficulty of getting news in the first place, the costs of production, the dependence on subscribers, and the limits imposed by business necessity—what is extraordinary is the vitality, the fearlessness, and the polemical character of the colonial press. An examination of the press itself—newspapers and magazines, particularly—shows a general pattern of press freedom existing in reality if not in law. To concentrate on cases of intimidation without reference to the general environment of journalistic energy out of which they emerged is to distort the picture of what the press was really like in colonial America.

Anyone examining the early history of American journalism is bound to be struck by the boldness of expression, the abundance of press controversy, and the frequent defiance of efforts to intimidate. Indeed, in at least one instance—the case of Andrew Bradford and the *American Weekly Mercury* of Philadelphia—a printer was unintimidated by arrest, and his paper apparently became more aggressive after the experience than it had been before. On September 18, 1729, the *Mercury* printed No. 31 of the *Busy Body* series, which stressed the dangerous tendency of public officials to perpetuate themselves in power. The essay, plagiarized from *Cato,* was offensive not so much for its sentiment as for its timing: It appeared just prior to the fall elections. The Council ordered Bradford held for examination and his printing office and home searched for evidence that would point to the author of the piece. The attorney general was instructed to commence prosecution. But all this seems to have had little effect on the printer. The following week the next installment of *Busy Body* appeared as before, more outspoken than ever. The author explained that he "had not enlarg'd lessened or altered [the essay], for what has happened upon Publishing the other." Bradford was soon released from custody, but his brief scrape with the authorities apparently had the opposite effect from that which was intended; "from this time forward the *Mercury* was bolder than ever" (Mott, 1962:25).

In the 1830's, Bradford fought a running battle against Andrew Hamilton, the powerful speaker of the Pennsylvania Assembly. On matters of defense policy, the *Mercury* took the side of the governor, who urged more strenuous measures than the pacifist-minded, Quaker-dominated House was willing to accept. And Bradford defended the governor's Chancery Court in 1735, at a time when it was under attack by Hamilton and the legislature. The *Weekly Mercury* defended the executive establishment, but it was by no means a conservative journal. In taking on Andrew Hamilton and the Assembly, Bradford was challenging the real political power center in Pennsylvania and, in the aftermath of Zenger, the body most likely to oppress him.

Another illustration of press controversy in Pennsylvania deserves closer analysis. William Smith (not the same William Smith who was involved with William Livingston and the *Independent Reflector*) first came to Philadelphia from New York in 1753. A native of Scotland and soon to be ordained as an Anglican minister, Smith was interested in promoting higher education. His proposals regarding the Academy and Charitable School in Philadelphia led to his appointment as its first provost when the institution became a college in 1755. Smith's ambitions, however, went beyond educational innovations, and he quickly became the most controversial political and literary figure in the city. His relationship with Benjamin Franklin, Philadelphia's leading citizen, had been close at first; Franklin was instrumental in securing Smith's appointment to the College. Their political differences soon drove them into opposing camps, however, and the breach in their relations lasted throughout their lives.

The backdrop for the developing political controversy in Pennsylvania was the French and Indian War, the great contest between France and England for imperial dominion in North America. Smith assumed his teaching duties in the Philadelphia Academy in the spring of 1754, about the time when hostilities between the French and the British commenced along the Pennsylvania frontier in the Ohio Valley. The English cause did not go well in the early years of the struggle. Washington's surrender at Fort Necessity in July, 1754, followed a year later by General Braddock's disastrous defeat in the battle before Fort Duquesne, gave the French control of the strategic upper Ohio region until November, 1758. During this interval, the fate of Pennsylvania as an English colony was in doubt. The French menace, coupled with a breakdown of the traditionally amicable relations between the Pennsylvanians and the neighboring Delaware and Shawnee Indians, threatened the very life of the province and seriously challenged the pacifist policies of the dominant Quakers.

The great questions confronting the political leadership of Pennsylvania during this crucial period related directly and immediately to defense. Above all, two measures were required if the colony was to meet its military responsibilities—an adequate supply bill and an effective militia act. Like so many other issues in colonial politics, however, these became intertwined with the on-going contest between the executive and the legislature for control of provincial government. The Assembly was willing to pass the requisite military measures, provided that, in doing so, it did not enhance the powers of the governor of the colony. Specifically, the Assembly demanded that the proprietor's estates, like all other property, be subject to tax in the general revenue measure it was being called upon to enact. This the governor, Robert Hunter Morris, refused to do, since it contravened the specific instructions he had received at the outset of his administration. The governor and the Assembly remained deadlocked on this question even after Braddock's defeat. Morris would not accede to Assembly demands, but until he did so, the Assembly would refuse him his militia bill. By the fall of 1755, however, action could no longer be postponed. Indian marauding on the frontier in October led to a march on Philadelphia by irate frontiersmen. The Assembly was forced to respond.

The result was a series of compromises between the governor and the Quaker party. A revenue measure was passed, with proprietary estates still exempt from taxation; but an Assembly commission was authorized to superintend the expenditure of funds. A militia act provided that men could claim exemption from service on grounds of conscience and that company officers were to be elected by enlistees. Finally, in 1756, the Assembly passed, over Quaker opposition, a mutiny act for the purpose of establishing some discipline in the militia.

To some extent Quaker religious principles explain the half-heartedness of the war measures undertaken by the Pennsylvania Assembly in 1755 and then again in 1756, but just as important was Assembly fear that any concessions would mean surrender of constitutional authority to the executive. Historically, executive power increased in time of war because of increases in expenditures and military formations under executive control. The Pennsylvania Assembly was determined to prevent the war from undermining its constitutional position in this way. Robert Hunter Morris was replaced, in the summer of 1756, by William Denny, a man of less ability and insubstantial political connections. The result was that, despite the war crisis, the power of the Assembly relative to that of the governor was never greater than during the emergency of the middle 1750's.

William Smith moved into the eye of the storm lashing Philadelphia's political life within a year of his taking up permanent residence in the city. He became the voice of the proprietary faction—a loose coalition of men and interests bent upon overturning Quaker power in the Assembly. As an Anglican ecclesiast, Smith sided with anti-Quaker religious groups, the Presbyterians in particular. He enthusiastically supported the appointment of an Anglican bishop for the Americas. In addition, in the crisis of the empire, Smith championed strong measures to deal with the French and Indian threat. Early in 1755, reacting to the French occupation of Fort Duquesne on the upper Ohio, Smith composed one of his most controversial political essays: *A Brief State of the Province of Pennsylvania* was published in London but widely circulated in Philadelphia. In it, Smith suggested that members of the Assembly should swear an oath declaring allegiance to the King and a willingness to take all necessary measures to defend his interests—in effect, a call to Quakers to resign from legislative office. In addition, Smith urged that the German residents of the colony be disfranchised, at least temporarily, and that they be barred from public office. As the German Pietist sects were allied with the Quakers, this was another way of striking at Quaker power. *A Brief State* elicited considerable opposition, much of it either written or inspired by Franklin; Smith responded the following year in a pamphlet called *A Brief View of the Conduct of Pennsylvania in 1755*, a sequel to his earlier work. He "seems to have been constitutionally incapable of resisting an impulse to 'sound off' in public controversy" (Ketcham, 1963:143).

The recently enacted militia law calling for the election of officers had led to Franklin's elevation to the command of the Philadelphia Regiment. Franklin was now at the zenith of his political power. Though not totally in support of the Quakers' halfway defense measures, he was still their most influential spokesman and defender. Governor Morris organized an independent militia company known as the "Association," as a counterweight to Franklin's regulars. The rivalry between the regular militia and the "independents," between the Assembly and the governor, and between Franklin and Smith erupted in William Bradford's *Pennsylvania Journal*, already the leading voice of opposition to Assembly measures and the long-time competitor of Franklin's more conservative *Pennsylvania Gazette*, which did the printing for the government.

Smith's attacks upon the Quaker-dominated Assembly for the inadequacy of its defense policy eventually led to a summons to appear before the bar of the House. But he refused to be humbled by this encounter and came out with a new pamphlet, *Obadiah Honesty*, in which he upheld the freedom of the press. Smith's printer, on the other hand, one James Chattin, *was* intimidated, and he refused thereafter to print or sell any more of Smith's inflammatory essays. Undeterred, and supported throughout by the trustees of Philadelphia College, provost Smith found another instrument for broadcasting his controversial views. William Bradford, grandson of the pioneer American printer, and nephew, adopted son, and apprentice to Andrew Bradford, whose *American Weekly Mercury* had established a tradition of newspaper radicalism in Philadelphia a generation before, became Smith's close ally.

Bradford agreed to publish a periodical that Smith would edit. They called it the *American Magazine and Monthly Chronicle for the British Colonies*. Although it lasted for only a year, it was to become the "most vital and original literary magazine published in America before the War of the Revolution" (Richardson, 1931:99). The first installment appeared in November, 1757. In it, Smith reprinted a recent English militia law, a scheme for establishing an effective militia in Pennsylvania, and an essay that argued that, while militia forces were adequate for general purposes, only hired mercenaries were equipped to deal with marauding Indians. The rest of the magazine was devoted to literary and scientific pieces. The most important, from a political point of view, was an essay by the "Antigallican" that bemoaned, in Spartan spirit, the effects of luxury and ease upon civil society.

On January 6, 1758, William Smith was arrested, cited for contempt, and denied relief on a habeas corpus petition by order of the Assembly. He remained in prison until the adjournment of the house in April and then, in September, was rearrested for a brief period of internment until the Assembly was dissolved. Smith thereupon sailed for England to press his appeal for redress before the Privy Council.

The ostensible reason for Smith's arrest was his support of one William Moore, a justice of the peace in Chester County. Moore's hostility to the ruling Quaker party was long-standing. As far back as July, 1740, Moore, then an Assemblyman, had antagonized the Quakers by denouncing their refusal to vote supplies to prepare for possible military operations during King George's War. In 1755, with Pennsylvania again faced with a military crisis, Moore had renewed his urgings with the Assembly for the enactment of a strong militia law to deal with Indian raids. On August 25, 1757, Moore was called to appear before the House to answer charges of misconduct in office, but he refused to comply and issued a statement denying that the Assembly had the power to try him as if it were a judicial body. The Assembly and Moore both appealed to the governor, William Denny, each charging the other with malicious behavior.

Moore was finally arrested with Smith, Moore for libeling the House in his petition to the governor and Smith for publishing the petition in a German newspaper, although it had already appeared in the official *Gazette*. The governor was sympathetic to the two men and criticized the Assembly for neglecting urgent matters while engaging "in new heats and disputes, at a time when public danger surrounds us on every side." The governor dismissed all charges against Moore in August, 1758.

Meanwhile, Smith continued to bait the Assembly from the

jailhouse. The February, 1758, issue of the *American Magazine* contained a statement by Moore and most of the relevant public documents in the case, including lengthy communications between the governor and the Assembly. Even more significant, however, was the first appearance at this time of the "Watchman" epistolary essays in Bradford's *Journal*. There is a little doubt that Smith was the author of this series. In defense of Moore, the "Watchman" argued that even the House of Commons itself did not have the power to act in a judicial capacity against an official charged, as Moore had been, with extortion. In addition, the essay quoted generous portions from Cato's strictures on press liberty.

At least two of the "Watchman" letters appeared in the *Pennsylvania Journal* while Smith was still confined. Letter III was republished in April, the month of his release, in the *American Magazine*. Here, Smith commented upon the "uncommon endeavors used, for a number of years past, to overawe the Press, and to vilify and intimidate the advocates for *impartial Enquiry*." The third "Watchman" also contained a letter, supposedly written by a Quaker, that declared that the Friends should not have aspired to rule if they were unprepared to employ the instruments of power. It concluded with the charge that the troubles of Pennsylvania were caused by "men who have their own selfish schemes to pursue."

"Watchman" VI appeared in the *American Magazine* in June. It began on a sharp note of alarm: "There never was a time when activity, diligence, and attention to public affairs, were more necessary than for some years past in this province; and yet no time, perhaps, when less were to be found." In general, the essay was a philosophical discourse analyzing the failings of men in power. There was no mistaking its intent, however, or the immediacy of its application. It charged those to whom power had been given with selfishness and neglect of the public good.

In July, Smith reprinted the seventh installment from his "Watchman" series, this time a statement on how the cunning and stratagems of "weak and wicked rulers" seek "to suppress all inquiries into their conduct." Smith's description of the techniques of repression had a striking resemblance to his own experiences as a victim of the legislature's animus. His readers did not have to be alerted to the connection. Of the evil of men in power, he wrote:

> They will always look on the friends of truth, as their own particular enemies. If you examine their conduct, they will be angry, because they know, you must blame. If you blame, they will punish cruelly, because they know, the censure of the just, and are certain that if they cannot put a stop to all enquiries by acts of severity, they themselves soon come to condign punishment. Whence, every word will be termed *"seditious,"* every truth *"libellous."* To tell, what you know, will be call'd "false"; to speak what you think, *"villainous."* When matters come to this pass, Genius will be depressed, Freedom of speech and writing banished, Honesty tongue-tied, and then commences all the political process of *seizing, examining, imprisoning, burning,* and what not [p. 495].

Smith described how the ancient Athenians spent public funds for festivals and merriment while Philip of Macedon approached their city in strength. "Nothing was more true, than that they were running into destruction; and yet nothing more dangerous than to tell them so." Lest the ancient analogy, however heavily drawn, escape his readers, Smith applied it to present circumstances with breathtaking force and bluntness:

> At the commencement of those murders and outrages [by the Delawares and Shawnees] under which this unhappy country now bleeds, in a certain province we all know [Pennsylvania], tho' like the *Athenians,* they had no law absolutely converting their public revenues to rioting and excess, yet they [the people of Pennsylvania] had plåced all confidence and authority in men, whose avowed principles forbid their converting it to that which is its real use . . . repelling violence and protecting the innocent from blood and slaughter. Nothing was more certain than that the continuing power in such hands [the presently constituted Assembly], tended to increase the public calamity, and to let in total destruction and distress upon the community. And yet nothing was more dangerous than to say so.

These were defiant words for a man recently imprisoned for an attack upon the legislature.

In August, the "Watchman's" eighth letter, a direct attack upon the people's representatives, appeared in the *Pennsylvania Journal*, and was reprinted in the *American Magazine* soon after. Popular rulers needed to be watched more than traditional tyrants, Smith argued, for by linking their names and their interests together with that of the people they manage to camouflage their own sinister designs. The "Watchman" warned that "no people ought to entertain such an exalted opinion of the abilities or integrity of their rulers, as to approve of every thing they do; without ever suspecting they are capable of error or deceit." He advised his countrymen to pursue wiser policies than those heretofore followed and to get rid of "all those . . . whose weakness, wickedness, or malice render[s] them unfit for the sacred trust consigned to them."

August, 1758, saw the last appearance of the "Watchman" in the *American Magazine*. Smith was returned to jail in September. In December, he sailed for England, not as an exile or political refugee but as a petitioner demanding vindication from the only power capable of granting it—the King in Council. In England, Smith was celebrated by the Anglican hierarchy for his activities in the colonies. His strong support for the imperial cause naturally earned him great favor. The Privy Council finally cleared him on a nice legal point. The law officers of the Crown recommended that Moore's address to Governor Denny, which Smith had published, was indeed libelous, but that only the Assembly so libeled could act upon it; Smith's arrest by a subsequent Assembly was therefore unlawful.

Vindicated, Smith returned to Philadelphia early in 1759. His career as an educator, minister, and essayist was far from over. He opposed the Stamp Act in 1765 and the oppressive measures of the mid-1770's that led to the break with England. He remained a loyalist, however, and, despite the unpopularity of such sentiments in the winter of 1775–76, he was unafraid to publicize them. His *Plain Truth* pamphlet answered Thomas Paine's advocacy of independence in *Common Sense*. Its appearance at the height of the Revolutionary crisis, along with other articles by Smith and fellow moderates advocating reconciliation, is another example of the Philadelphia press keeping pace with the continuing vigor of public debate.

Smith's *American Magazine* and Bradford's *Pennsylvania Journal* in the stormy period of the French and Indian Wars together illustrate a side of American journalism in the colonial era that deserves more study and appreciation. The actions of the Pennsylvania Assembly against Moore and Smith represent another example of how legislatures rather than courts had become the agencies for press suppression in the period after Zenger, with "breach of privilege" replacing seditious libel as the major offense charged. But Smith's encounters with the Assembly—like Moore's—did not intimidate him. During his first imprisonment, he began composing the "Watchman" essays for the *Pennsylvania Journal,* and upon his release he reprinted them in the new *American Magazine.* He remained unintimidated by the Assembly, despite the fact that his position was counter to that of the leading oligarchs of Philadelphia—the Quakers and their supporters—and directly affronted perhaps the most powerful legislative body in all America. To be sure, Smith left for England as a direct result of his incarceration, and the effect of his departure was to terminate the life of his monthly journal. Still, by that time the worst of the military crisis had passed. In November, 1758, the French abandoned Fort Duquesne, and the threat to the life of the colony—which Smith had laid to Quaker vacillation—was ended. But in the months that counted, Smith wrote and published material offensive to the Assembly. His position was not vindicated by an early change in public attitude, for the Quakers remained the dominating force in Pennsylvania politics until the Revolution. But, in retrospect, his activities do help to rescue the reputation of the editors, writers, and printers of the period.

IV

A close examination of political controversies in other colonies would show that we need to revise our image of the colonial press. New York maintained a spirited, politically oriented press after the Zenger trial. In the early 1750's, one of the most colorful and animated debates occurred over the founding of King's College, later Columbia. The controversy centered around a major magazine, the *Independent Reflector,* and several minor satellites that had spun off from it—among them, the *Occasional Reverberator* and *John Englishman.* Hugh Gaine's *New York Mercury* was the *Reflector's* chief antagonist. Unlike William Smith's *American Magazine and Monthly Chronicle* in Philadelphia, the *Independent Reflector* did not challenge the provincial Assembly head on, but the explosion it ignited shows that the press in New York provided a more than adequate forum for the discussion of highly sensitive and divisive public questions.

Even when the power of the Assembly did come into play, it does not seem to have deterred adverse commentary. James Parker was called to account in 1756 for publishing news reports that the Assembly interpreted as slurs upon its reputation, but in 1759 Parker published a broadside challenging the wisdom of New York's recently enacted stamp duty on legal documents and newspapers—a more directly aimed criticism. Probably because it failed to produce sufficient revenue to justify keeping it, the impost was dropped. Still, the importance of the episode is not to be measured by the effect or lack of effect Parker's statement had but by the fact that he spoke out at all. A printer intimidated by fear of reprisal would hardly have questioned the good sense of the legislature in imposing a highly controversial tax. Moreover, the 1759 broadside was only the last of Parker's remonstrances on this issue. Back in 1756, when the measure was still under consideration in the legislature, Parker had written an article in his *Post-Boy* denouncing the proposed levy.

A final example, also from New York, points out the futility of legislative attacks upon the press. In the famous McDougall case of 1769–71, it is clear that the effort to punish McDougall for criticizing the New York Assembly was "counterproductive," in that his incarceration broadcasted to the other colonies the wrongheadedness of the Assembly's action in voting supplies for British troops and stimulated a major press war that further publicized McDougall's criticism of the legislature. The "Dougliad" essays, defending the Assembly and attacking McDougall, appeared in Hugh Gaine's *New-York Gazette and Weekly Mercury* in the spring of 1770, but anti-Dougliad rejoinders were printed in the *New York Journal* and the *New-York Gazette or Weekly Post-Boy*. McDougall contributed to the controversy from his prison cell. Legislative repression, like the license laws and court trials of an earlier era, seem to have had little effect in curbing press freedom.

Recent studies indicate just how important the press was in shaping American consciousness not only during but even long before the Revolutionary crisis itself. Richard L. Merritt (1965), a penetrating student of the press in the pre-Revolutionary period, has shown that a sense of an American identity preceded the institutional formations that followed quickly upon the break with England. What Merritt calls the "symbols of American community" were evident in the press in the generation before the great political upheaval of the mid-century. Not pale and anemic but healthy, controversial, and strong, American journalism reinforced an emerging American consciousness and brilliantly reflected the vitality of American political life. As James M. Smith (1963) has suggested, despite seditious libel, "there was almost certainly a much wider degree of freedom of expression in colonial and early national America" than we have been led to believe. The law, after all, responds to social reality as much as it shapes that reality. It was the tension between seditious libel and legislative privilege, on the one hand, and the fact of a vigorous press, on the other, that ultimately brought the law into line with the substantial press freedom that prevailed in colonial America.

6

The Character of Politics

I

In some ways, colonial politics prefigured American political experience in the years to come. Colonial public life was rich in controversy, political institutions were surprisingly open, and participation in government at some levels was widespread. To be sure, there are marked differences between the political attitudes and campaign practices, and the values and goals of public life then and now, and these need to be noted. But politics nourished the roots of colonial constitutionalism even as the health of the political system today is our surest safeguard that constitutional government will continue.

One of the great debates in American history in recent years has focused on the extent to which colonial America was a political democracy. Historians are divided on this question into at least three camps. Some have said that it was not democratic, some that it was; others have attacked the appropriateness of the question, asserting that it is foreign to the concerns of the colonial American. The literature on this debate is already extensive, and there is no need to review it again. It might be useful, however, to focus upon some of the relatively undisputed claims in the controversy and apply them to a reconstruction of the most important features of colonial political life in general.

It does appear that the right to vote was extensive among adult white males in the colonial era. Chilton Williamson, whose

129

history of the suffrage (1960) is the most comprehensive modern treatment we have, estimates that between 50 and 75 per cent of the free, adult white males over twenty-one could vote in colonial America. Both in local and in colonywide elections, qualifications to vote for town selectmen, for "select" vestries, and for deputies to the provincial assemblies were either easily satisfied or ignored altogether. Normally, qualifications to vote were based on the possession of real property, but because of the wide availability of land, these were not serious impediments to the establishment of a fairly broad electorate. In Virginia, possession of real property either as a freehold or as a lease for life or lives was the prerequisite for the voting franchise, but townsmen could also vote if they owned a dwelling and a piece of a town lot. However, slaves or other forms of movable or personal property, regardless of value, did not suffice. Elsewhere, the distinction between real and personal property did not obtain. In Massachusetts, a man's property had to be worth £40 sterling; in Connecticut, £40 in current money. Landed property was not required in either province.

More important as a barrier to voting than property restrictions were the physical encumbrances connected with voting procedures. Usually, the poll was taken at the county seat, which meant that some voters living in very large counties had to travel many miles at considerable personal sacrifice to exercise their franchise. Time off from work meant several days or more lost at the harvest or in the planting season. Overnight stays in highway inns while en route were costly. Even to vote in town elections could prove burdensome. Some New England towns encompassed a number of scattered and separate villages, only one of which was designated as the polling place, and voters might have to travel a considerable distance in order to vote.

Because of the physical hardships that attended voting in some localities, there was a natural tendency for candidates to encourage their known supporters to go to the polls by offering to pay at least some of the costs of food, drink, and, if necessary, lodging along the way. In most colonies, however, statutes prohibited candidates from "treating" voters in these ways prior to the election once the governor had issued the writ of election. In Virginia, such electioneering practices were strictly limited by law, and no candidate could give money, food, entertainment, gifts, contracts, or promises of favor without running the risk of disqualifying himself from office. *The Concessions and Agreements of West New Jersey* (1677) provided that "no person or persons who shall give bestow or promise directly or indirectly to the said parties electing any meat drinke money or moneys worth for procurement of their choice and consent shall be capeable of being elected a member of the said Assembly." Nevertheless, these laws were often evaded, and "treating" was widely practiced. Supporters performed the customary catering services, thus relieving the candidate himself of direct legal liability. Given the difficulties, burdens, and costs of traveling to the polls, voters came to expect some type of recompense, but once the proscriptions of law set in, the "treat" was confined to food and drink offered at or near the poll at the time of voting. Meals, lodging, travel costs, and other expenses for voters residing at a distance became their own responsibility.

Besides the inconvenience, cost, and lost labor time that voting often entailed, the voter also opened himself to various forms of physical and moral intimidation when he went to the polls. Supporters of one candidate might deliberately attempt to impede voters known to favor another. There are cases of blocked roads, of bridges torn down, and of ferry boats wrecked to prevent opposing voters from reaching the county seat. If all else failed, an outright brawl might be set off at the voting place. Pennsylvania elections were known for their turbulence, and voters were sometimes warned to come armed to the polls. In Philadelphia, rival factions fought openly to "control the stairs" leading to the poll in the central market in 1738. The "trial of the stairs" was an accepted feature of Philadelphia voting practice. The Philadelphia election riot of 1742 occurred because of special anxieties and tensions, but disorders of this kind were not uncommon in port towns because of the presence of voteless seamen, who often had a stake in the outcome of a local election.

The difficulties of voting rather than qualifications controlling the right to vote explain why some elections were poorly attended. Voters were normally apathetic. Unless the election was hotly contested or the issues were of particular interest, voters preferred to stay home. Voting, however, was not a right or a privilege; it was a civic duty, like militia service. The law not only entitled freeholders to vote; in some colonies, freeholders were penalized if they did not. Virginia imposed a fine of 200 pounds of tobacco if a voter failed to go to the polls. In seventeenth-century Plymouth, freemen were fined for not attending town meetings or for not voting for the town's deputies to the General Court—two reasons why freemanship was not always enthusiastically sought after in that colony. In Massachusetts, towns that dodged the responsibility (and the cost) of sending at least one deputy to the legislature were subject to a stiff penalty.

The county sheriff was the principal officer charged with conducting the election procedure. He voted only in cases of a tie and was expected to conduct the proceedings impartially. Yet, he rarely maintained a neutral posture. A sheriff could determine the outcome of contested elections in some provinces by neglecting to notify voters in areas where sentiment was opposed to his own, by moving the poll to another location at the last minute, by excluding qualified and admitting unqualified voters, by closing the poll after those he favored had voted, by filing incorrect returns, and, finally, by intimidation. A voter who supported candidates whom the sheriff opposed could very well find himself called with bothersome regularity to jury duty, a civic responsibility even more onerous than voting itself.

The voting process itself tells us much about colonial political attitudes and behavior. The voters assembled *en bloc* on the common or before the county courthouse, and when the vote was called they divided according to their choice. The sheriff could decide by visual estimate—"upon the view"—whether there was a unanimous vote, or else which group was larger and, therefore, which candidate was chosen if there were more than one. If many candidates were running, or if an election was vigorously contested, a "poll" of the voters might be required. Each man would then be called by name to step forward and either declare his vote aloud, or submit a written ballot with his own name affixed thereto, or make his selection in a more secret manner. Pennsylvania tried to establish a kind of secret ballot:

Each voter dropped a bean into a divided container; sometimes different-colored beans were used for different candidates. In most colonies, however, voting was open. To announce one's vote aloud and without fear was a mark of civic pride.

II

These practices seem unsophisticated and replete with faults and weaknesses to us, and yet colonial Americans probably considered them about as fair, valid, important, and liberal as we do ours. Take, for example, the property qualification itself. To us, any kind of property test for voting is a deprivation of a basic human right; it seems to favor the haves and discriminate unjustly against the have-nots. Men in the eighteenth century, however, did not view it this way. The property restriction was a device—originally a liberal reform—for preventing local men of wealth, power, and influence from controlling the outcome of elections. Given that most voting was oral and that a man's choice was public knowledge, it was necessary to insulate the voter as much as possible from social pressure. A tenant was not very likely to risk his lease by voting against the known inclinations of his landlord; nor would an apprentice or bound servant vote against his master or a debtor against his creditor. The theory was that tenants and servants, like women, slaves, and children, did not have "wills of their own," and only a man with a minimum of property was sufficiently self-possessed to exercise a free choice. Even though, in reality, tenants often voted with surprising independence, it was believed that, in the absence of a property qualification, the rich and powerful would be able to march to the polls at the head of a parade of dependents prepared to vote at their dictation.

Property qualifications, therefore, were thought to minimize outside pressure and equalize power among the electorate, just as property qualifications for office were originally designed to reduce the officeholder's incentive to use his position for personal gain. Historians have tended, by implication, to applaud the fact that the property qualification was not important because it was frequently ignored, the result being to enlarge the size of the voting population. But it is possible that elections in which voter qualifications were not examined may have been less "liberal" than those in which they were. "Fagot voting" and "colonizing" were the terms used to describe customs whereby temporary deeds of property were given to unqualified voters so that they could satisfy eligibility requirements and then vote the way of their benefactors. Such blatant efforts to manipulate elections led to the establishment of residency qualifications and hikes in the minimum amount of property needed to vote. For example, Virginia first defined the size of the minimum freehold necessary to vote in the 1736 reform law—one hundred acres of unimproved land of twenty-five acres with a house and plantation—to offset the recently discovered tendency of the rich to lease small parcels of land in return for support at the polls.

The property qualification was also justified on the basis of the "stake in society" theory. Since taxes on real property were the principal source of government revenue, and as English law and tradition dictated that taxes were the "free gift" of consenting freeholders, it followed that taxpayers alone were entitled to vote for officials charged with raising and disbursing public funds. On the basis of such logic, plural voting made good sense. If a freeholder owned land in more than one county or election district, he ought to vote as many times as he was subject to tax. In fact, it was considered an abuse of a voter's privilege if a sheriff in one county called for an election on the same day as that in another county, since this could well deprive freeholders with sufficient land in each of their lawful right to vote twice. Above all, the property qualification for voting tended to limit the electorate to a body of men sharing those traits of character that property ownership—freehold ownership, in particular—were said to reinforce: independence, stability, reliability, honesty, and integrity. In short, as Chilton Williamson (1960:5) has suggested, such qualifications made farming virtues into political virtues.

The whole question of secret voting as opposed to public voting also needs some rethinking. To colonial Americans it was by no means obvious that secret voting was superior to oral voting. There were (and are), after all, certain hidden costs. Secret ballots were by no means immune to manipulation. If the results of a secret ballot were challenged, a new vote was required. In colonial times, this was a considerable hardship: Voters had already been inconvenienced once and were unlikely to undertake the tedious, time-consuming, and costly journey to the poll a second time. A secret ballot would require the validation of all voter qualifications prior to the election, an additional burden to an already encumbered system. Americans knew about secret voting—it was provided for in the *Concessions & Agreements of West New Jersey* and it was required by law in Pennsylvania and the Carolinas—but there was no significant agitation for it during the colonial era except in New York. On the other hand, an oral vote was less subject to dispute. Each voter's choices were listed next to his name. It was a simple task to recheck the result by going through the poll. If an unqualified voter was on the list, his vote could be crossed off without affecting the validity of the entire canvass.

III

If colonial voting habits appear quaint to us, their campaign techniques are remarkably less so. Discounting the obvious differences occasioned by modern communications media and transportation technology, the attitudes and practices of colonial nominees running for office parallel our own in a number of interesting and even striking ways. While it was not considered good form to trumpet one's personal assets as a candidate, those who did not were often repudiated at the polls. The accepted conventions of politics required that a man "standing for election" demurely await the judgment of his character by his fellow citizens, but reality dictated that a serious politician actively solicit votes and advertise his candidacy by appearing at the polling place on election day. Personal contact was the most effective way of winning support. People voted as much on the basis of a personal evaluation as on issues. A candidate who was widely known, who managed to visit voters throughout the election district, who shook hands, knew the family, and remembered the names of the children was likely to be more successful than the self-effacing gentleman who stayed at home. Many public men lamented the necessity of having to appeal to the people, but they performed the required rituals or risked voter rejection.

In addition to personal contact, politicians used the public prints extensively. Pamphlets, broadsides, reprints of the Assembly *Journal,* and letters to the editors of newspapers were the accepted and frequently employed techniques for broadcasting the virtues and positions of one candidate as opposed to the failings of another. Whispering campaigns, rumor-mongering, and slander were not considered to be in good form, but they were also not uncommon. In addition, voters were persuaded—at a price—either to vote in support of a particular candidate or to withhold support from an opponent by not voting. These kinds of practices were best known in the most politicized of the colonies. Elections in New York, prior to 1765, were controlled by "bosses" who rounded up voters by direct or indirect bribes and conducted extensive "paper wars" in the press—all of which was financed through well-stocked campaign treasure chests. In Pennsylvania, the dominant Quakers, more a political than a religious group by the 1750's, used the annual Quaker meeting as a caucus for choosing nominees for the Assembly. "Tickets" were put together and printed, and there is even some evidence of ethnic balancing to attract immigrant votes.

Patronage of one sort or another was also used to collect votes. A member of the Boston delegation to the Massachusetts House of Representatives instructed James Otis, Jr., on how he should conduct his first campaign for election by telling him his own experience:

> I can also tell you, by way of example, some of the steps I take: two or three weeks before an election comes on, I send to the cooper and get all my casks put in order: I say nothing about the number of hoops. I send to the mason and have some job done to the hearths or the chimneys: I have the carpenter to make some repairs in the roof or the wood house: I often go down to the ship yards about eleven o'clock, when they break off to take their drink, and enter into conversation with them. They all vote for me. [Cited by Robert Zemsky, *Merchants, Farmer, & River Gods,* 1971:243].

All these techniques—campaign literature, trips around the circuit, buying up votes, carefully distributing patronage in the right places—were expensive. In most instances, the candidate had to have either resources of his own or the support of wealthy patrons.

By the end of the colonial period, a surprisingly modern political *system* had developed in a number of colonies. Rhode Island, the most independent-minded and autonomous province, was also among the most politicized. "Proxy" voting—a system whereby the voters submitted printed ballots in their respective towns, which were then forwarded to Newport for tabulation in the General Court—required a high degree of political organization. Each of the two rival factions that dominated Rhode Island politics in the generation before the Revolution caucused to decide on nominees, printed proxy "tickets," organized newspaper campaigns, and sent speakers and "runners" around the province to drum up and hunt for voter support. "Rhode Islandism" came to be used throughout the colonies as a term of derogation, describing practices that were thought to demean public life but were increasingly discoverable in places other than Rhode Island itself.

The sum of the parts of colonial electoral practices from campaign to election may not add up to democracy. The historians who have criticized the "colonial democracy" school are certainly right in asserting that Whiggism, deference, and the need for consensus explain more about early American political culture than its putative democratic character. Still, we must not underestimate either the degree of public participation or the effects that such participation had upon colonial public life. It was, as Chilton Williamson (1960:42) has said, an "age still predemocratic in its conscious thought, although not in many of its practices and institutions." Those who were white, male, propertied, and Protestant who could and did vote in colonial elections were deferential to their "betters" and expected the "natural leaders" of the social order to control the administration of government. But they also had a lively sense that their vote counted—as it surely did in an electorate of limited size, where elections often turned on a handful of votes in a canvass of a few hundred—that their needs and desires deserved recognition, and that candidates who failed to defer to the people ought not to be returned.

IV

A clear example of the relationship between the voters and their representatives is the Land Bank controversy in Massachusetts in 1740–41. One of the major economic problems facing colonial America was the chronic shortage of an adequate circulating medium of exchange. Many colonies—New England and the Middle Atlantic provinces, in particular—suffered from almost continuous trade deficits, which meant that specie coming into the country was siphoned off to make up for trade imbalances. Monetary tightness tended to deflate prices and depress business. In order to counteract these effects, colonial legislatures tried various inflationary experiments to increase circulation, raise prices, and discourage imports to the extent possible. The obvious and favorite technique was to print government paper. But the British Government and English merchants frowned upon paper money for the very same reasons that Americans applauded it: Business sluggishness and dear money meant greater profits for English merchants and manufacturers exporting to the American market.

In 1730, the Board of Trade decided to apply to Massachusetts restrictive policies in existence but unenforced for a decade. New paper issues were to be limited and outstanding notes retired in order to return the province to a specie-based currency within ten years. The new directive had explosive potential. During the 1730's, Governor Jonathan Belcher disregarded Board of Trade instructions and continued to allow paper issues, but toward the end of the decade he began to move toward compliance with royal policy. Large segments of provincial opinion looked upon his growing commitment to financial retrenchment as fraught with disaster. By 1740, a political deadlock between the governor and the inflationists in the Massachusetts House of Representatives brought the province government near paralysis. The financial problem had become a burning public issue.

At this point, one John Colman revived a scheme that had
been in circulation in Massachusetts for nearly a century and
had already been used, with some success, in other colonies. Colman suggested the establishment of a private credit bank based
on land mortgages. His proposed "land bank" would issue circulating notes redeemable in twenty years and payable in commodities or company bills. It was a simple device by which land—
Massachusetts' major natural resource—would be used as a basis
for a needed medium of exchange. The Land Bank and Manu-
factory Scheme promised to solve the problem of insufficient currency, low prices, excessive imports, and a lagging economy.

Colman's Land Bank quickly became the central political issue in Massachusetts. Some Boston commercial interests tried to
set up a silver bank as a conservative alternative to the Land
Bank, but the idea had little support. The Land Bank was popular with a broad cross-section of the electorate, and in the spring
election of 1740 a lower house dominated by Land Bankers was
returned that proceeded to protect the Bank from executive
interference. In September, 1740, the Bank issued its first paper
notes. Belcher and the Massachusetts Council attempted to out-
law the Bank by executive proclamation, but this served only
to polarize political alignments even more.

In May, 1741, Land Bankers again won in the provincial elections. The "Land Bank House" proceeded to take reprisals against
the Council—a body chosen by the House of Representatives—
which had sided with Belcher in his attempt to destroy the Bank.
Sixteen councilors were purged, but the governor responded by
dissolving the new Assembly. Soon afterward, partly as a result of
a petition filed by Massachusetts merchants, Parliament quashed
the Bank by applying the Bubble Act of 1720, which proscribed
speculative enterprises. In addition, William Shirley was appointed to replace Belcher as provincial governor. In the ensuing
months, Shirley managed to work out a series of compromise
measures by which the Bank was liquidated with a minimum of
hardship and inconvenience to its subscribers.

The political fall-out resulting from the Land Bank explosion was considerable. John Adams once remarked that the tur-
moil in Massachusetts over the Land Bank exceeded that which

followed the Stamp Act a generation later. But what is of special interest here is how the controversy illustrates the relationship between public policy and voter behavior. There was an increase in the number of representatives sent to the General Court from towns usually too apathetic or parsimonious to send their full quota of deputies. For example, the number of deputies to the House of Representatives sent by Worcester county towns doubled between 1739 and 1741. Land Bank supporters throughout the province beat the bushes for voters with striking results. Robert Zemsky estimates that, despite what would be a normal "nonreturn rate" of 33 per cent over the ten-year period 1739–49, 70 per cent of the deputies from conservative regions of Massachusetts failed to be re-elected in 1741, the year when elections to the General Court were a virtual referendum on the Land Bank scheme. In contrast, more radical regions, whose deputies generally supported the Land Bank, saw the nonreturn rate for 1741 fall to 29 per cent from what would be a ten-year average rate of 34 per cent. George A. Billias (1959:42), a student of the Land Bank controversy, concludes that it "roused the colonists from their apathy and spurred them into political action. The rising tide of voters mustered by the land bankers threatened to engulf the royal governor and to upset the established pattern of government."

The elections to the House of Representatives in 1740 and 1741, when the Land Bank agitation was at its height, clearly demonstrated that, in Massachusetts, the political system was capable of responding to a vital public question. Uncontested elections and elections involving insignificant public issues brought few voters to the polls. But when elections mattered, the electorate acted. Such was the case in the money crisis of Massachusetts in the 1740's, but a similar condition could be found in most of the other provinces. Issues of genuine importance generated meaningful divisions and gave a "surprisingly democratic, even modern cast" (Williamson, 1960:47) to politics. Public-policy questions of sufficient moment significantly affected voter behavior. The electorate was an important variable in government. Colonial political life may not have been democratic, but it did stimulate a political process characterized by frequent elections, competition for office, development of issues, and exposure of official conduct to public scrutiny. Government was not just a matter of administration by "the better sort." Through political activity, the notion of responsible government, responsive to an enlarged and critical public, was gaining ground.

V

If colonial political life was based on an unusually broad and active electorate, it found its expression in those constituted bodies that actually governed. On the provincial level, the most important of these was the colonial assembly, the focal point of colonial political activity and the central concern of political ideologues. The assemblies represented the voice of the people in the government itself, guarding popular rights and properties and preventing the executive from overstepping his constitutional authority. They were looked upon as the mediating force between the "rulers" and the "ruled." But representatives were also quasi magistrates. Once elected they were, as a part of the government, rulers worthy of obedience. The only check upon their abuse of authority was the electoral process itself. In the power to vote, the people retained some ability to pass upon the performance of their deputies. Thus, colonial constitutional ideology consisted of a series of checks—that of the legislature upon the executive; that of the people upon their delegates. Colonial political and social thought was essentially adversarial: The few checked the one, and the many checked the few.

Here again, however, the reality of colonial politics differed from prevailing notions of what political life should be about. If theory posited a politics of popular deference to the wisdom of society's natural leaders, the practice of representative politics was much more assertive, interest-oriented, and independent. As Bernard Bailyn (1967:chap. 5) has shown, the tradition of requiring deputies to represent the expressed wishes of the community in the legislature—or pay the price of subsequent repudiation by the voters—goes back to the medieval notion of attorneyship: The legislator was, in effect, a spokesman for the people who had deputized him to plead their cause before the King in Council; he was not a free agent sent to legislate according to his conscience. At a time when the role of the English parliamentarian was moving closer to the latter, more modern definition of the representative function, the Americans were in the process of resurrecting the older view of the delegate as advocate. During the crisis of the Revolution, these opposite interpretations of the legislator's role were to achieve a clear-cut definition: *virtual representation* (the English view) versus *actual representation* (the American view). It is clear, however, that the ideologues of the Revolution merely conceptualized the role of the people's deputy as it had come to be known through the collective experience of most of the mainland provinces.

Colonial legislative representation was characterized by residency requirements—a deputy normally had to live, or at least own property, in the district he represented; by "binding instructions"—a deputy was told what course of policy he was to pursue, at first only with regard to local issues, then on public questions of intercolonial concern; by accountability—a deputy's performance in the legislature was measured by the extent of his adherence to his instructions. As stated in Chapter 35 of the West New Jersey *Concessions and Agreements:*

> That the said Proprietors and Freeholders at their choice of persons to serve them in the Generall and Free Assemblys of the Province give their Respective Deputies or Trustees their instructions at large to represent their grievances or for the improvement of the Province and that the persons chosen doe by indentures under hand and seale Covenant and oblidge themselves to act nothing in that capacity but what shall tend to the fitt service and behoofe of those that send and employ them and that in case of failer of trust or breach of Covenant that they be questioned upon complaint made in that or the next Assembly by any of their respective Electors.

To be sure, these elements of the representative function were not universal. The residency requirement obtained in only nine of the mainland colonies; the practice of instructing deputies seems to have been articulated earliest in New England and was less well established in the Middle and Southern Colonies. Yet, even in Virginia, where politics was more staid, where traditional behavioral norms survived longest, and where the politics of deference was more deep-rooted because of the relative stability and homogeneity of the ruling gentry—even there, a growing effort to bind the delegate to the wishes of his constituents is discernible. The question was debated in the House of Burgesses in 1754. As Landon Carter, a leader of the Virginia gentry, defined it, the issue was "whether a representative was obliged to follow the directions of his constituents against his own reason and conscience or to be governed by his conscience." For the most part, however, Virginians continued to reject the practice of instructing delegates at least until the Revolution. "Instruction was hardly compatible with deference" (Pole, 1966:163).

In another important way, colonial representative assemblies reflected the activism and assertiveness of American politics. In comparison with the English Parliament, the lower houses of assembly were fairly well apportioned according to population. Until the end of the colonial period, the Board of Trade made no serious effort to restrict their size. As a result, new towns in New England and new counties elsewhere continued to gain representation in the assemblies to the extent desired without much difficulty. Studies of Massachusetts, New York, New Jersey, Pennsylvania, and Virginia show that legislatures were fairly well apportioned. Indeed, direct representation of specific property interests—as opposed to numerical and regional representation—appears to have emerged only later and as a consequence of conservative fears for the rights of property excited by the passions of the Revolution.

The very character of the colonial assembly (its representativeness) and the nature of the colonial legislator's function (to be an advocate for his constituency) helps to explain why, in most colonies, political activity concentrated on the legislature. Legislators were close to the people. Assemblies contained elements from the different sections of each province. Where regional, economic, ethnic, and religious differences were sharp—as, for example, in New York, Pennsylvania, and Massachusetts—these differences were reflected in the political struggles for membership in, and control of, the provincial legislatures. Where, on the other hand, a colony, however large, had an undifferentiated economy and a relatively homogeneous population—as in Virginia—political activity in the legislature was less likely to be unhinged by permanent factions separated by differences on fundamental issues. Here, personal rivalries and transitory squabbles —surface divisions—tended to be the rule. But most assemblies, in the generation before the Revolution, were not so tranquil as the Virginia House of Burgesses. Society in most of the mainland provinces in the late colonial period was increasingly fractured by class polarization, religious feuds, ethnic suspicions, and economic competition among rival interests. This social diversification was reflected in political life, particularly at the provincial level. Political factionalism was becoming the most salient feature of American politics.

The emphasis upon factional as opposed to class antagonisms is one of the trademarks of recent colonial historiography. Richard Buel, Jr. (1964:167), refers to the "seething, factionalism of provincial politics." Bernard Bailyn (1968:63–64) writes of "chaotic factionalism," which he explains as follows:

> There was bitter, persistent strife within the provincial governments almost everywhere. There was strife, first of all, between branches of government—between the executives on the one hand and the legislatures on the other—strife so rampant as to be more noteworthy by its absence than its presence and so intense as to lead on occasions to a total paralysis of government. But it was not only a matter of conflict between branches of government. There was, besides this, a milling factionalism that transcended institutional boundaries and at times reduced the politics of certain colonies to an almost unchartable chaos of competing groups.

In short, colonial Americans were—to use a phrase that Patricia Bonomi (1971) has applied to New York, but which has even more general utility—a "factious people."

Evident of this factiousness is to be found in the growing body of detailed political studies of individual colonies. Reviewing this literature in a very comprehensive essay, Jack P. Greene (1966) has attempted to establish a working "typology of political forms" that helps to put the discrete experiences of the separate provinces into comparative perspective. Greene denotes four descriptive categories or models: (1) *chaotic factionalism*—a political condition beset by shifting and evanescent alliances among competing groups; (2) *stable factionalism*—on-going rivalry among more permanently divided elements; (3) *domination by a single, unified group*—interludes of relative calm brought about by the emergence of a ruling elite that effectively curbed factional forces; (4) *faction-free, with a maximum dispersal of political opportunity within the dominant group*—a variation of category 3 wherein competition was kept within the confines of a large, open, and relatively homogeneous oligarchy rooted in a stable and well-integrated social substructure. According to Greene, individual colonies did not adhere to only one of these models but often shifted from one to another. So, for example, before the abrogation of its charter in 1684, the pattern of politics in Massachusetts is best described by model 3; from 1684 until the Land Bank controversy and the ascendency of William Shirley in 1741, by model 1; from 1741 until 1760, factionalism in Massachusetts again was held in check; and, from 1760 until the Revolution, the pre-existing, single-group dominance gave way to the stable factionalism of model 2. What is significant in Greene's analysis, in addition to its originality and breadth of focus, is his substitution of faction for class as the major analytical device for comprehending colonial politics. According to his scheme, the presence (or, for that matter, the absence) of faction becomes the central feature of colonial political experience.

The causes of faction in colonial America were many. As Bailyn has pointed out, in addition to the regional, economic, and ethnic divisions already referred to, faction resulted when political weakness at the executive level of colonial government stimulated a struggle for power in the assembly among society's elite, itself a shifting group of competing claimants for social and political pre-eminence. The assemblies not only seized prerogatives traditionally assigned to the executive but also granted favors in the distribution of land, awarded contracts for the construction of internal improvements, allotted privileges and monopolies, and regulated economic activity and trade. The needs of the povinces, as new societies, were great. In satisfying those needs, the assemblies had to expand the scope of governmental functions beyond traditional limits, thereby increasing legislative competence and the stakes of politics.

VI

Political factionalism was widespread in colonial America. Historiographical efforts to explain its causes have deepened our understanding of the structure of colonial politics, the forces that propelled it, and the way politicians worked. There is, however, one side to faction that needs to be examined, for it helps to untangle the confusion of thought and practice that, to some extent, has muddled our understanding of the colonial era.

In theory, political activity of the sort described in these pages was not accepted as part of the normative processes of government in the well-ordered state. Rather, it was the sign of division and disaffection, a sign of a lapse in government itself. Politics was not, as in modern liberal culture, an integral part of constitutional government; it was its antithesis. The idea that government was a prize to be fought for by contentious groups was opposed to the purposes for which government was established. Government was the embodiment as well as the servant of society. Its chief end was the promotion of the common good, or "commonwealth." As the Reverend John Wise put it in a searching essay (*Vindication of the Government of New England Churches*) in 1717:

> A Civil State is a Compound Moral Person whose Will is the Will of all; to the end it may Use, and Apply the strength and riches of Private Persons towards Maintaining the Common Peace, Security, and Well-being of all. Which may be conceived as tho' the whole State was now become but one Man.

Representation was desirable precisely because it improved the chances that government would encompass and comprehend the interests, and thus the good, of all.

This dominant ideology did not allow for the participation of particular groups, or "parties," in government itself. For particularism was opposed to the general good. To introduce particularity, whether in the form of faction or of special interest, was to inject into the very councils of the state those noxious poisons that would open the body politic to the infection of private tyranny. As William Livingston put it in his essay on parties in the *Independent Reflector* (1753):

> Unspeakably calamitous have been the Consequences of Party-Division. It has occasioned Deluges of Blood, and subverted Kingdoms. It always introduces a Decay of publick Spirit, with the Extinction of every noble and generous Sentiment. The very Names of Things are perverted. On Fury and Violence it bestows the Appellation of Magnanimity and Opposition, and stiles Resentment and Rancour, Heroic Ardor, and Patriot-Warmth. Nor is it ever at a Loss for Pretences to bubble the Mob out of their Wits, and give its wildest Ravings a plausible Colour.

Party and faction were a blight. Outside the government, they fomented discord; inside, corruption and tyranny. The well-ordered polity was free of "party spirit."

Despite this prevailing antiparty ideology, however, colonial politics was riven with passionate political controversy. In almost every colony, "factions" were the most visible feature of the political landscape. Well-meaning governors were badgered by them on almost every issue of substance. Those public matters requiring legislative consideration and concurrence, such as tax policy, appropriations, fee schedules, salaries, the establishment of courts of justice, and the regulation of the militia, usually elicited vigorous public debate. Factions representing different groups and opposing points of view were strong in the legislative assemblies. Governors decried the "baneful effects of the spirit of party," but they, in their turn, had to join one of the existing groups or else organize a "governor's party" to counteract this pernicious influence.

This peculiar discrepancy between an antiparty, antifaction ideology and a well-developed, rapidly maturing, and highly volatile political life could not last indefinitely. Political activity was inevitable, given the nature of colonial institutions, the fairly wide exercise of the franchise, the comparative openness of

American society to political ambition, and the ever increasing size of the representative assemblies—that natural breeding ground for political controversy. As a result, the conventional wisdom was becoming less and less relevant to the realities of eighteenth-century political life. The first fissures in the wall of ideological orthodoxy were at least visible near the end of colonial times. Wherever faction enlivened politics, men were forced to confront the discrepancy between a prevailing anti-party ideology and the on-going existence and utility of party and faction in daily political life. Indeed, in those provinces where factionalism was pervasive, the illogic of the conventional wisdom concerning politics was first perceived.

Not surprisingly, one of the earliest manifestations of a new concept of oppositional politics appeared in the *New York Weekly Journal* at a time when its illustrious printer, John Peter Zenger, was in jail awaiting trial. A lead article on March 17, 1734, began with proper obeisance to standard formulations of the accepted wisdom:

> Factions and Parties in a State, or any other Society, are no Doubt very pernicious. . . . He must therefore have very little public Spirit, or even Humanity, who . . . fully either kindles or foments such cruel Disorders in his Country.

Clearly, the writer—probably the editor, James Alexander—agreed that political factionalism was an evil, and that society ought to be rid of it. The remaining portions of the essay, however, are more enigmatic; essentially, they modify the initial theme:

> But however inconsistent with Goodness and Virtue, it is to take a Pleasure in the Divisions of Ones Country, or to be active in the Promoting of them we ought not to extend this so far as some do, who upon such Occurences give Themselves Airs of being intirely distinterested, and disclaim all Attachment to any of the contending Parties in a State.

Party may be bad, but it is not the worst of evils. To feign disinterest while pursuing party purposes is to aggravate the bad effects of political divisions:

It may therefore be of some Use to enquire, how far an honest Man in a Time of public Dissentions ought to embark in them, and take part in the Debates relating to them, so as to discover his Opinions and Inclinations for one Party or Principle more than another.

Better to own up to one's particular position than to dissemble. What has a public man to hide? Each man, after all, conceives his own cause to be good, not evil:

If we are engaged in a good Cause, and I fancy no Man willingly espouses what he thinks a bad one, what should make us either ashamed or afraid of owning our Affection for it?

Moreover, not only is it better to declare one's position openly; it may be unrealistic to suppose that a disinterested position is possible:

. . . it is impossible for a Man who converses at all in the Wourld, to conceal his Sentiments about any Maner of Importence which happens to be agitated in it. And therefore none should aim at a Qualification which cannot be attained without impairing their Virtue.

The *Weekly Journal* did not state that "party spirit" was good, only that "public spirit" may not be possible and that it is better to air the diversity of men's views than to attempt to disguise them behind masks of pretended virtue. Man has the right "freely to examine and debate all matters either in Philosophy or Religion."

Two other examples are illustrative of the new trend of thought. Both are products of the cacophonous 1750's. One is an outgrowth of the fight in New York over the establishment of King's College—later Columbia—as an Anglican school; the other, the result of William Smith's paper war against the Quakers in Pennsylvania. In his essay on parties in the *Independent Reflector*, William Livingston managed to stake out new ground after reiterating the standard conventions of his time. In its concluding portion, Livingston argued that harmony in government *was not* a sign that all was well in the well-ordered state!

> It must after all be allowed, that a long and uninterrupted Calm in a Government divided into separate Branches, for a Check on each other, is often presumptive, that all Things do not go well. Such is the restless and aspiring Nature of the human Mind, that a Man intrusted with Power, seldom contents himself with his due Proportion. For this Reason, an unremitted Harmony between several Persons created as a Counterpoize to each other, is suspicious. Their Union may be the Consequence of their keeping within their proper Limits, and it may be the Effect of an iniquitous Coalition.

From here, Livingston proceeds to draw out the implications of this logic. If a false tranquillity in government may camouflage hidden motives and sinister designs, then healthy conflict and vigorous dissent in society at large may better preserve the liberty of the subject:

> To infer, therefore, that the Liberties of the People are safe and unindanger'd, because there are no political Contests, is illogical and fallacious. Such a Tranquility may be the Result of a Confederacy in Guilt, and an Agreement between the Rulers to advance their private Interest, at the Expence of the People. But this can never be our Case. Agreeable to the generous Spirit of our Constitution, we have a Right to examine into the Conduct and Proceedings of our Superiors; and upon discovering them in a Combination of Roguery, if we cannot set them together by the Ears, we can form a Party against their united Strength: And such a Party, I hope we may never want the Spirit to form. To conclude, shou'd a future Governor give into Measures subversive of our Liberties, I hope he will meet with proper Opposition and Controul.

Thus, the evil spirit of party might capture men in government as well as men out of government. The separation of the branches of government was not an ironclad warranty against such an occurrence. The formation of a party outside the government to counteract factious elements within was, therefore, justified.

The Fathers of the Republic would later compose, in Richard

Hofstadter's efficient phrase, a "Constitution against parties"; the principal device they would employ to render party useless was to be the separation-of-powers principle. Only afterward would it be realized that separation of powers was, in itself, not sufficient, and that party was a vital extraconstitutional check upon tyranny. William Livingston's prophetic essay, written in 1753, anticipated this realization by at least half a century.

William Smith's essay "On the good and ill Effects of civil DISSENTION," published in the very first edition of the *American Magazine and Monthly Chronicle* (1757–58), justified in advance the oppositional stance that that periodical would assume throughout its brief career. It also mirrored the growing awareness of the existence of faction and the need to legitimize the reality of political conflict. As the "Planter" argued in a bold formulation of the new theory:

> . . . political evil, internal discords, and civil commotions, which threaten the dissolution of a state, are frequently no more than the efforts of the constitution to expel certain noxious principles, and the proper effect of them is to establish the public weal in a more vigorous, regular and permanent state. . . . [H]appy is the state which is informed by it in the requisite degree. Its operation is salutary; and the consideration of this has often lighted up the hopes of the patriot.

It is a brilliant statement. Faction is no longer the source of social decay but a sign of health—it is society purging itself of "noxious principles." Smith suggests that political dissent may not be merely an acceptable evil but a "salutary" and even necessary thing if the public good is to be made "vigorous, regular and permanent."

To be sure, political dissension has evil effects if pushed to extremes. Developing the medical metaphor, a favorite literary conceit of the period, Smith explains just why party can exist only in the "requisite degree":

> . . . *Dissensions* in a state, . . . are productive sometimes of good, sometimes of evil effects. They resemble a fever in the human body, the general intention of which is salutary; namely, by the

increased action of the solids and fluids upon each other to expel
the morbific matter, which has disordered the constitution, and to
restore the animal machine to its wonted health and vigor. Yet such
may be the violence of the conflict, as intirely to destroy the functions of some principal organs; or, carried to a still greater height,
to bring on a dissolution of the whole fabric.

Smith has not completely abandoned the old ideology. Dissent,
like fever, has bad as well as good effects. Nevertheless, he has
departed from convention in significant ways. He has recognized
that, willy-nilly, political dissent and division will exist everywhere. It is part of the design of God, Nature, and the Universe
—indeed, dissension is as necessary to liberty as fever is to health,
and as moral evil is to virtue:

> . . . collisions are more or less the fate of every State; that they
> discover the defects and weak sides of a government to those who
> had delayed repairing and fortifying them, for no other reason
> than that they had not before the same opportunity of knowing
> them; that they give a clearer insight into the constitution, make
> people examine and understand their rights and liberties, and
> thereby teach them where to stand upon their guard against
> attacks from abroad, as well as the no less dangerous reforms of
> pretended patriots at home.

The modalities of colonial political life were tied to the past.
Politics was viewed in traditional terms: It was the conflict between the government and the governed. In the context of the
Anglo-American world, this was perceived as a fundamental struggle between the royal prerogative and its vice-regents, on the one
side, and representative assemblies, on the other. The political
conflicts that resulted from this polarization were not viewed as
normative but as extraordinary conditions occasioned by dis-
equilibrium among the branches of government. In the well-
balanced state, politics was not only unnecessary, it was unde-
sirable. At the time of the Revolution, many believed that, once
the colonial governors were stripped of their arbitrary powers,
the basis for further political conflict would dissolve and the long-
sought unanimity of interest and opinion so fundamental to the
commonwealth idea would finally be achieved.

But the highly factious politics to be found in most colonies, some more than others, gave the lie to these traditional notions. Nor would political conflict diminish with the coming crisis of the Revolution; it would, in fact, intensify. And as it intensified, the antiparty ideology of the earlier period would become increasingly irrelevant to the emergent reality—now visible to all—of continuing and deeping party conflict.

The colonial political process consisted of many components: interest-group representation, deference toward popular opinion, the development of vote-getting procedures, and ideological movement toward new concepts of oppositional politics. Political institutions—factions, in particular—began to have a life of their own; that is, like modern parties, the interest of the factions began, in some places, to transcend the particular issues, personalities, and interests that had given them birth. Recent emphasis on the pervasive Whiggism and the "politics of deference" in the late colonial period—a welcome reaction to the excessive claims of the "colonial democracy" school of historical thought—has partially obscured the vigor and the surprisingly mature state of development that colonial politics had reached. For, long before the Revolution, Americans had achieved "political competence" (Bonomi, 1971:281); the "public accepted the reality and pertinence of political conflict" (Katz, 1968:48). Not only did America *have* a political culture; increasingly, America *was* a political culture—discrete in its separate provincial parts but sharing common experiences; above all, sharp, often fierce, political battles resolved by political procedures of astonishing modernity.

7

The Colonial Constitution in Retrospect

What, then, was the measure of colonial constitutionalism? To what degree did public life in colonial America match up to the model of constitutionalism described in the first chapter of this book? The evidence is neither altogether uniform nor absolutely conclusive. Yet, on the basis of the analysis presented here, it should be clear that a fairly strong case can be made for a substantial colonial achievement in these areas.

Colonial Americans had a keen sense that they possessed the important legal safeguards that were the ornaments of English law. From the very beginning, the concern that procedural regularity and substantive liberties should be protected by written codes, charters, and statutes and recognized in the ordinary course of law and justice was a central one. Of course, large segments of the population—slaves, bonded laborers, the poor— would have been hard put to discover the existence of these liberties in their daily lives. Moreover, the scope and definition of civil liberties were much more circumscribed then than they are now. But from the perspective of the eighteenth century rather than the twentieth, what is extraordinary is the liberality of of American law, the important position this liberality occupied in the system of justice, and the degree to which it equaled and at times surpassed the English experience, which was thought to be the most enlightened in the Western world.

In the field of religion, there was a remarkable and unique recognition of the need to invent new relations between church and state. Practical necessity was the overriding impulse behind America's religious liberalism, but idealism and theory had a role to play, too. By the end of the colonial period, America had reached a turning point in church-state relations. The old definitions were clearly obsolete, while newer ones, such as multiple establishment, failed to have the durable stability that single establishment had supplied for so long. Separation of church and state was not achieved by the end of the colonial period, but weakened church establishments were visible all across the mainland. The right to worship freely—or not to worship at all—and to act on the basis of one's private religious beliefs—which American republicans looked upon as the very essence of freedom—was widespread.

As for the press, there is substantial evidence that, in reality, it was much more open and uninhibited than the law would seem to have permitted. Undoubtedly, some editors and printers were intimidated by the threat of prosecution and imprisonment for seditious libel or for breach of legislative privilege. Yet, where controversy over public issues was sharp, there does not appear to have been an absence of acerbic press commentary. Our traditions of courageous and competitive journalism do go back to colonial America, where the reality of journalistic freedom was stretching and breaking the old legal parameters of permissible utterance.

Finally, recent work in the field of provincial politics shows lively and vigorous conflict, the beginnings of modern notions of the place of politics in free government, and the emergence of new ways of conducting political activity and new standards of political behavior. Here again, the colonial period did not witness the completion of these developments—only their beginnings. The emergence of the colonial assemblies—the principal but by no means the only institution of government that provided a forum for registering the will and gaining the consent of the people—gave provincial politics focus and importance. Politics had become sufficiently mature and the assemblies sufficiently developed to lay the basis for political independence, to carry

the Revolution through to successful completion, to organize new
governments, to write and adopt workable constitutions, and to
prevent anarchy on one side and oligarchical tyranny on the
other. These tasks took courage, wisdom, and experience, all of
which the colonial political system was able to produce.

Recent work in social history would suggest that so positive
an interpretation of our colonial past ought to be viewed with
skepticism. Class polarization, racial oppression, social immo-
bility, growing economic deprivation—the themes of important
recent studies—raise questions as to the value and significance of
civil, religious, press, and political freedom in the context of
social and racial inequality. The questions are valid but somewhat beside the point. Social justice is a goal that liberal
societies have pushed to the forefront of public consciousness
in the twentieth century, just as in the nineteenth century they
fought for democracy and in the eighteenth for individual liberty. Perhaps, as M. J. C. Vile (1967:349) suggests, "It is natural
that the emphasis upon [this] one value, social justice, [is] so
great in a period when the realization of the shortcomings of
earlier ages in this respect [has] become so intense." Social justice
is among the basic goals of our collective life, and it is fair to
suggest that, to the extent that our constitutional regime fails
to achieve this end, it fails to fulfill its deepest promise and its
fundamental purpose. But social justice, as we know it, was not
cherished as a basic value by colonial Americans. To argue
against calling their regime "constitutional" because it did not
promote tasks that we, more than two centuries later, consider
central, is to distort colonial America's real achievement and
its primary contribution to the betterment of man.

In our own time, intimidation of the press, illegal arrests and
mass internments, the use of a standing army to suppress peaceful demonstrations of dissent, prosecution of the leaders of unpopular causes, illegal break-ins by government agents, ominous
increases in official surveillance, deliberate attempts to subvert
the political process, the failure of the government to prosecute
officials for unlawful acts—these are more than minor aberrations.
They represent serious breakdowns in the constitutional order

itself. Yet, the institutions of our constitutional system—the press, the parties, the courts, the other organs of government—are sufficiently energetic for us to conclude that, despite these lapses and excesses, we still live under a constitutional regime. Constitutionalism is our best and safest foundation for dealing with the social ills that beset us. It is, after all, primarily out of our constitutional tradition that the notions of social justice and equality that we as a people profess have emerged. Constitutionalism supplied to colonial Americans the values, the tools, and the assurance that enabled them to respond to tyranny when they perceived it. We, too, draw upon that rich legacy when we respond to threats to liberty in our own time—threats that early Americans would have understood, and which they taught us how to meet.

Bibliographic Essay

In organizing the secondary materials needed in the preparation of this work, I have leaned heavily upon the excellent compilation by Jack P. Greene, *The English Colonies in the Eighteenth Century, 1689–1763* (New York, 1969), one of the Goldentree Bibliographies in American History. Greene's book of documents, *Settlements to Society, 1584–1763* (New York, 1966), is the most comprehensive collection of primary materials available in one volume. The reader should also be aware of basic source collections not limited to single colonies: Francis N. Thorpe (comp.), *The Federal and State Constitutions, Colonial Charters, and Other Organic Laws . . .* (7 vols.; Washington, D.C., 1909); Benjamin P. Poore (comp.) *The Federal and State Constitutions, Colonial Charters, and Other Organic Laws of the United States* (2 vols.; Washington, D.C., [1878]); and Leonard W. Labaree (comp.), *Royal Instructions to British Colonial Governors, 1670–1775* (2 vols.; New York, 1935).

1. Introduction: Constitutionalism in the American Experience

My thinking about the subject of constitutionalism has been shaped by a number of important works. Carl J. Friedrich's classic *Constitutional Government and Democracy: Theory and Practice in Europe and America* (rev. ed.; Boston, 1941) emphasizes the theme of limitation and restraint and considers modern constitutionalism in relation to a host of subjects. Charles H. McIlwain's thought-provoking little book, *Constitutionalism: An-*

cient and Modern (rev. ed.; Ithaca, 1947), illustrates the problems of constitutionalism in various historical periods and, in particular, challenges the central role we in America have assigned to separation of powers and checks and balances in modern times. F. D. Wormuth's *The Origins of Modern Constitutionalism* (New York, 1949) shows the transition from medieval to modern constitutionalism, particularly in seventeenth-century England.

Several of the themes I have selected for my model are derived from materials collected in, and introduced by, C. Peter Magrath in *Constitutionalism and Politics: Conflict and Consensus* (Glenview, Ill., 1968). In emphasizing the importance of the "independence" of church and state, I am following the position taken by John C. Bennett in *Christians and the State* (New York, 1958) and Leo Pfeffer in *Church, State and Freedom* (rev. ed.; Boston, 1967). On the central importance of political action and political responsibility as elements of modern constitutionalism, see Herman Belz, "Changing Conceptions of Constitutionalism in the Era of World War II and the Cold War," *The Journal of American History*, LIX (1972), 640–69.

Another way of constructing a model for modern constitutionalism—one that makes a case for the continuing validity of formal constitutional structures and divided power, recognizes the importance of a vigorous press and political parties, and defends the whole notion of constitutionalism against behaviorist emphasis on process as opposed to form—is to be found in M. J. C. Vile, *Constitutionalism and the Separation of Powers* (Oxford, 1967), especially chap. 12. For an approach to the origins of American constitutionalism that stresses notions of fixed fundamental law, the compact theory of government, natural rights, Puritan theology, and the common law, see Andrew C. McLaughlin's still challenging *Foundations of American Constitutionalism* (New York, 1961). Finally, Lawrence H. Leder, in *Liberty and Authority: Early American Political Ideology, 1689–1769* (Chicago, 1968), examines most of the issues considered in this book and attempts to reconstruct the public's attitude toward the salient constitutional questions facing colonial Americans.

2. THE COLONIAL CONSTITUTIONAL STRUCTURE

There are numerous works on the structure of the early empire. For a general overview, see A. B. Keith, *The Constitutional History of the First British Empire* (Oxford, 1930), chaps. 11–12, and Herbert L. Osgood, *The American Colonies in the Eighteenth Century* (4 vols.; New York, 1924], vol. I, chap. 1. For a short but useful introduction to the subject that summarizes much recent writing, consult Stanley N. Katz, *Newcastle's New York: Anglo-American Po'itics, 1732–1753* (Cambridge, 1968), chap. 1. Monographs on separate components of the imperial structure helpful in writing the text were Dora Mae Clarke, *The Rise of the British Treasury: Colonial Administration in the 18th Century* (New Haven, 1960), and I. K. Steele, *Politics of Colonial Policy: The Board of Trade in Colonial Administration, 1696–1720* (Oxford, 1968). For the later history of the Board, see Arthur H. Basye, *The Lords Commissioners of Trade and Plantations, Commonly Known as the Board of Trade, 1748–1782* (New Haven, 1925).

Evarts B. Greene's *The Provincial Governor in the English Colonies of North America* (New York, 1898; repr. 1966) is still the best introduction to the study of the role of the "executive," particularly in the royal and proprietary colonies. Leonard W. Labaree's *Royal Government in America: A Study of the British Colonial System Before 1783* (New Haven, Conn., 1930) is richer in detail but largely substantiates the thrust of Greene's book, which is that the general tendency of colonial government was toward the enlargement of assembly power. For an example of a study of a particular governor in one province, see John A. Schutz, *William Shirley: King's Governor of Massachusetts* (Chapel Hill, 1961). The governors' councils have not received attention comparable to that given to the other agencies of provincial authority—not surprisingly, in view of their position—but H. H. Bellot's "Council and Cabinet in the Mainland Colonies," *Royal Historical Society Transactions*, 5th ser., V (1955), 161–76, is extremely illuminating. Also worth consulting on this subject is Rex M. Naylor, "The Royal Prerogative in New York, 1691–

1775," in *Quarterly Journal of the New York State Historical Association*, V (1924), 221–55.

On the colonial legislatures, Mary P. Clarke's *Parliamentary Privilege in the American Colonies* (New Haven, 1943) is a detailed and fascinating analysis of the procedures and powers of the lower houses, dealing with such subjects as the assembly as court, the investiture of the speaker, the privileges of assemblymen, disputed elections, and so on. The book is basic to an understanding of assembly power. Clarke's work should be supplemented by S. M. Pargellis, "The Procedure of the Virginia House of Burgesses," *William and Mary Quarterly*, 2nd ser., VII (1927), 73–86, 143–57, which is pertinent for its detail on legislative procedure, its description of committee work, and its comparisons with English legislative practice. The process by which the assemblies "rose to power" in particular provinces is detailed in the definitive statement of the "assembly encroachment" thesis, Jack P. Greene's *The Quest for Power: The Lower Houses of Assembly in the Southern Royal Colonies, 1689–1776* (Chapel Hill, 1963). J. R. Pole's important book, *Political Representation in England and the Origins of the American Republic* (New York, 1966), supports this point of view in most particulars. The major challenge to the "assembly encroachment' interpretation is John M. Murrin's interesting article, "The Myth of Colonial Democracy and Royal Decline in 18th Century America: A Review Essay," *Cithara*, V (1965), 53–69. Murrin does not dispute the "rise to power" of the assembly, but he pushes it farther back in time and questions one important part of the thesis, namely, that assembly ascendancy necessarily meant gubernatorial decline—a view, he proposes, with which most contemporaries would not have concurred. The more moderate positions referred to in the text were stated in Robert Zemsky, *Merchants, Farmers, and River Gods: An Essay on Eighteenth-Century American Politics* (Boston, 1971); Stanley N. Katz, *Newcastle's New York;* and Bernard Bailyn, *The Origins of American Politics* (New York, 1968). For one study of a lower house, see Lucille Griffith, *The Virginia House of Burgesses, 1750–1774* (rev. ed.; University, Ala., 1968). George E. Frakes shows the importance of the committee system in the growth of the power, competence, and capacity for self-government of the lower house in one colony in *Laboratory for Liberty: The South Carolina Legislative Committee System, 1719–1776* (Lexington, 1970), especially chap. 2.

Finally, for purposes of comparing the lower houses with the House of Commons, see P. D. G. Thomas, *The House of Commons in the 18th Century* (New York, 1971), and Sheila Lambert, *Bills and Acts: Legislative Procedure in 18th Century England* (Cambridge, England, 1971). Useful discussions of the place acts are to be found in E. Neville Williams, *The 18th Century Constitution, 1688–1815: Documents and Commentary* (Cambridge, England, 1960), and Betty Kemp, *King and Commons, 1660–1832* (New York, 1957). The best treatment of the meaning of "mixed government" in England is Corinne C. Weston, *English Constitutional Theory and the House of Lords, 1556–1832* (New York, 1965).

There is a growing body of authoritative literature on the subject of the colonial judicial systems. For an extremely useful survey that details the different types of courts, see Erwin C. Surrency, "The Courts in the American Colonies," *American Journal of Legal History*, XI (1967), 253–76, 347–76. For an incisive analysis that focuses on important questions, such as common-law reception, jurisdictional lines, and review procedure, see Julius Goebel, Jr., *History of the Supreme Court of the United States: Antecedents and Beginnings* (New York, 1971), chap. 1. The whole subject of equity law and equity courts in relation to salient political-constitutional questions is interestingly considered by Stanley N. Katz in "The Politics of Law in Colonial America: Controversies Over Chancery Courts and Equity Law in the 18th Century," *Perspectives in American History*, V (1971), 257–84. The complicated story of the fight over equity in New York is analyzed by Joseph H. Smith and Leo Hershkowitz in "Courts of Equity in the Province of New York: The Cosby Controversy, 1732–1736," *American Journal of Legal History*, XVI (1972), 1–50. For the reasons why separate equity courts were not established in Massachusetts, see Edwin H. Woodruff, "Chancery in Massachusetts," *Boston University Law Review*, IX (1929), 168–92, and William J. Curran, "The Struggle for Equity Jurisdiction in Massachusetts," *Boston University Law Review,* XXXI (1951), 269–96.

The background for the U.S. Constitution's provisions governing the federal judiciary is analyzed by Martha A. Ziskind in "Judicial Tenure in the American Constitution: English and American Precedents," *Supreme Court Review* (1969), 135–54. Ziskind's conclusion that the Constitution precluded judicial removal by legislative address ought not to be accepted without consulting Raoul Berger's *Impeachment: The Constitutional Problems* (Cambridge, Mass., 1973), chap. 4. The controversy over tenure "during good behavior" can be followed for New Jersey in Donald L. Kemmerer's "Judges' Good Behavior Tenure in Colonial New Jersey," *New Jersey Historical Society Proceedings,* LVI (1938), 18–30; and for New York, in Milton M. Klein, "Prelude to Revolution in New York: Jury Trials and Judicial Tenure," *William and Mary Quarterly,* 3d ser., XVII (1960), 439–62.

The comprehensive role of the county court in local government in colonial Virginia is examined in detail in A. O. Porter, *County Government in Virginia: A Legislative History, 1607–1904* (New York, 1947), chaps. 1–2, and Isabel Ferguson, "County Courts in Virginia, 1700–1830," *North Carolina Historical Review,* VIII (1931), 14–40. For North Carolina, see William C. Guess, "County Government in Colonial North Carolina," *James Sprunt Historical Studies,* XI (1911), 5–39, and Paul M. McCain, "The County Court in North Carolina Before 1750," *Trinity College Historical Society Historical Papers,* ser. XXXI (Durham, 1954).

The best study of a high court of justice that considers all relevant matters—jurisdiction, powers, trial procedure, appeals, common-law reception, and so forth—is P. M. Hamlin and C. E. Baker, *The Supreme Court of Judicature of the Province of New York, 1691–1704* (3 vols.; New York, 1952–59), vol. I. The whole question of Privy Council disallowance of colonial judicial decisions and procedures is analyzed in Joseph H. Smith, "Administrative Control of the Courts of the American Plantations," *Columbia Law Review,* LXI (1961), 1210–53.

On the origin, development, and meaning of the doctrine of

separation of powers, two works are indispensable: W. B. Gwyn, *The Meaning of the Separation of Powers: An Analysis of the Doctrine from Its Origin to the Adoption of the United States Constitution* (Tul. Stud. in Pol. Sci., vol. IX, 1965); and M. J. C. Vile, *Constitutionalism and the Separation of Powers* (Oxford, 1967), which treats the subject comparatively and considers separation of powers in relation to the problems occasioned by the growth of political parties, the press, and administrative bureaucracy. The only book-length study of plural officeholding is Ellen E. Brennan's *Plural Office-Holding in Massachusetts, 1760–1780: Its Relation to the "Separation" of Departments of Government* (Chapel Hill, 1945). In my treatment of the place of the separation theory in the Revolution, I have followed Gordon S. Wood's analysis in *The Creation of the American Republic, 1776–1787* (Chapel Hill, 1969), chap. 4.

3. The Legal Rights of Early Americans

The literature in American legal history has grown in recent years, and the colonial period has received a large share of the attention of legal historians. A very good sampling of the kind of work that has been done is in David H. Flaherty's anthology *Essays in the History of Early American Law* (Chapel Hill, 1969). For an incisive review of the trends in historical writing in this field, see Stanley N. Katz, "Looking Backward: The Early History of American Law," *University of Chicago Law Review*, XXXIII (1966), 867–84. The "Anglicization" theme mentioned in the text is illustrated in John M. Murrin's "The Legal Transformation: The Bench and Bar of 18th Century Massachusetts," in Stanley N. Katz (ed.), *Colonial America: Essays in Politics and Social Development* (Boston, 1971), pp. 415–49.

The definitive work on the role of the Privy Council in controlling American legislative enactments and court decisions is Joseph H. Smith's *Appeals to the Privy Council from the American Plantations* (rev. ed.; New York, 1965); see also his "Administrative Control of the Courts of the American Plantations," *Columbia Law Review*, LXI (1961), 1210–53. The legal issues surrounding Calvin's case are also discussed in Sir William Holdsworth's *History of English Law* (16 vols.; London, 1903–66), vols. IX and XI.

Discussions of the formal enactment, codification, or adoption of legal guarantees of personal liberty can be found in Robert A. Rutland, *The Birth of the Bill of Rights* (Chapel Hill, 1955), chap. 2; A. E. Dick Howard, *The Road from Runnymede: Magna Carta and Constitutionalism in America* (Charlottesville, 1968); George Lee Haskins, *Law and Authority in Early Massachusetts: A Study in Tradition and Design* (New York, 1960); and Rodney L. Mott, *Due Process of Law* (Indianapolis, 1926).

Copies of the seventeenth-century constitutional enactments discussed in the text are reprinted as follows: The Massachusetts *Body of Liberties* is in E. S. Morgan (ed.), *Puritan Political Ideas, 1558–1794* (Indianapolis, 1965); The *Laws and Liberties* of 1648 are reprinted in Max Farrand (ed.), *The Laws and Liberties of Massachusetts* (Cambridge, Mass., 1929); the *Concessions and Agreements of West New Jersey* are included in Julian P. Boyd (ed.), *Fundamental Laws and Constitutions of New Jersey, 1664–1964* (Princeton, N.J., 1964). On particular questions related to these enactments, a number of essays are helpful. Richard B. Morris disputes the Bay Colony's contention that the *Body of Liberties* followed English law in "Massachusetts and the Common Law: The Declaration of 1646," *American Historical Review*, XXXI (1925–26), 443–53, reprinted in Flaherty (ed.), *Essays*, pp. 135–46. See Thorp L. Wolford's "The Laws and Liberties of 1648," in Flaherty, *Essays*, pp. 147–85, for the provisions of that code and for a discussion of the legal regime it inaugurated. The authorship of the *Concessions and Agreements of West New Jersey* is established by John E. Pomfret in "The Problem of the West Jersey Concessions of 1676–77," *William and Mary Quarterly*, 3d ser., V (1948), 99–102. On the development of the convention as a separate and special institution for constitution-making as opposed to ordinary law-making, see Gordon S. Wood, *The Creation of the American Republic, 1776–1787* (Chapel Hill, 1969), chap. 8. On the founding of Pennsylvania and the adoption of its *frames of government*, consult E. B. Bronner, *William Penn's "Holy Experiment": The Founding of Pennsylvania, 1681–1701* (New York, 1962). On the advanced definition of the "rights of Englishmen" reflected in New York's *Charter of Liberties,* see David S. Lovejoy, "Equality and Empire: The New York Charter of Liberties, 1683," reprinted in Katz (ed.), *Colonial America,* pp. 160–81.

County and superior court records for many provinces have been published over the past few decades. Most useful in the preparation of the text were P. M. Hamlin and C. E. Baker (eds.), *The Supreme Court of Judicature of the Province of New York, 1691–1704* (3 vols.; New York, 1952–59); Joseph H. Smith (ed.), *Colonial Justice in Western Massachusetts, 1639–1702: The Pynchon Court Record* (Cambridge, Mass., 1961); and Joseph H. Smith and Philip A. Crowl (eds.), *Court Records of Prince Georges County, Maryland, 1696–1699* (Washington, D.C., 1964).

Monographic studies of colonial courts and criminal procedure are numerous, but not all are of equal quality. The studies for New York are unsurpassed for their richness of technical detail. Besides Hamlin and Baker (ed.), *Supreme Court of Judicature,* vol. I, see Julius Goebel and T. Raymond Naughton, *Law Enforcement in Colonial New York: A Study in Criminal Procedure, 1664–1776* (New York, 1944). For Virginia, the old volume by Arthur P. Scott, *Criminal Law in Colonial Virginia* (Chicago, 1930), is still useful, and Hugh F. Rankin's *Criminal Trial Proceedings in the General Court of Colonial Virginia* (Charlottesville, 1965) is a colorful survey. Studies of crime and punishment for various colonies that contain some detail on criminal procedure are Raphael Semmes, *Crime and Punishment in Early Maryland* (Baltimore, 1938); H. W. K. Fitzroy, "The Punishment of Crime in Provincial Pennsylvania," *Pennsylvania Magazine of History and Biography,* LX (1936), 242–69; and H. B. Weiss and G. M. Weiss, *An Introduction to Crime and Punishment in Colonial New Jersey* (Trenton, 1960).

Leonard W. Levy's *Origins of the Fifth Amendment: The Right Against Self-Incrimination* (New York, 1968) is by far the best book about a particular civil liberty and encompasses much material about other legal rights as well. The extent to which New York recognized the privilege of not being forced to incriminate oneself under oath is argued by Levy and Lawrence H. Leder in "Exotic Fruit: The Right Against Compulsory Self-

Incrimination in Colonial New York," *William and Mary Quarterly*, 3d ser., XX (1963), 3–32. Studies of the legal rights considered in the text are Felix Rackow, "The Right to Counsel: English and American Precedents," *William and Mary Quarterly*, XI (1954), 3–27; Richard D. Younger, *The People's Panel: The Grand Jury in the United States, 1634–1941* (Providence, 1963), chap. 1; A. H. Carpenter, "Habeas Corpus in the Colonies," *American Historical Review*, VIII (1902), 18–27; Milton M. Klein, "Prelude to Revolution in New York: Jury Trials and Judicial Tenure," *William and Mary Quarterly*, 3d ser., XVII (1960), 439–62. That jury trials were not, however, customarily granted in criminal contempt cases is shown by Joseph H. Smith *et al.* in the appendix to the brief for the United States in *Harris* v. *United States* (382 U.S. 162 [1965])–a model historical study of a particular legal problem that also summarizes the principal materials showing the degree to which English common law was received in each of the Thirteen Colonies.

Finally, for a comparison of legal rights in America and England for this period, the reader should consult the classic study by Sir James F. Stephen, *A History of the Criminal Law of England* (3 vols.; London, 1883), especially vol. I.

4. THE RELATIONS BETWEEN CHURCH AND STATE

General works on church and state in American history abound. The standard treatise is Anson P. Stokes, *Church and State in the United States* (3 vols.; New York, 1950). Sanford H. Cobb's *The Rise of Religious Liberty in America: A History* (New York, 1902) has much detailed information but has been largely superseded by individual state studies, some of which are cited below. Evarts B. Greene's *Religion and the State: The Making and Testing of an American Tradition* (New York, 1941) is full of insight. Chapters 1–4 are still very useful for the colonial period. Fascinating statistical surveys plus an abundance of other data appear in E. S. Gaustad's *Historical Atlas of Religion in America* (New York, 1962).

Short interpretive works stressing such factors as geography, time, pluralism, and English imperial policy in forging the special relations between church and state that developed in America can be found in Sidney E. Mead, *The Lively Experiment: The Shaping of Christianity in America* (New York, 1963), especially chaps. 1–2; Timothy L. Smith, "Congregation, State and Denomination: The Forming of the American Religious Structure," *William and Mary Quarterly*, 3d ser., XXV (1968), 155–76; William W. Sweet, "The American Colonial Environment and Religious Liberty," *Church History*, IV (1935), 43–56; and Perry Miller, "The Contribution of the Protestant Churches to Religious Liberty in Colonial America, *Church History*, IV (1935), 57–66. The seventeenth-century origins of the notion of denominationalism is discussed by W. S. Hudson in "Denominationalism as a Basis for Ecumenicity: A Seventeenth Century Conception," *Church History*, XXIV (1955), 32–50.

General works with interesting information on church and state in colonial America are Robert A. Rutland's *Birth of the Bill of Rights, 1776–1791* (Chapel Hill, 1955), chap. 2 *passim*, and Lawrence H. Leder's, *Liberty and Authority: Early American Political Ideology, 1689–1763* (Chicago, 1968), chap. 3. Chapters 6–8 on church history in Richard Hofstadter's *America at 1750: A Social Portrait* (New York, 1971) luminously synthesize much of the new secondary literature.

The number of works on the Great Awakening is large and growing. Alan Heimert, in one of the more important recent books on the subject, *Religion and the American Mind: From the Great Awakening to the Revolution* (Cambridge, Mass., 1966), stresses its pivotal importance in shaping American religious and social thought for two generations. Heimert's position, however, is sharply criticized in a review by E. S. Morgan in *William and Mary Quarterly*, 3d ser., XXIV (1967), 454–59. C. C. Goen's *Revivalism and Separatism in New England, 1740–1800: Strict Congregationalists and Separate Baptists in the Great Awakening* (New Haven, Conn., 1962) is a detailed account of the emergence of the Separates from Congregationalism in the Great Awakening and their conversion to Baptism. The Separate Baptists were a major force in unraveling the web of the religious establishment in New England. On the transition from ecumenicism to denominationalism in the Awakening, see Dietmar Rothermund, "Political Factions and the Great Awakening," *Pennsyl-vania History*, XXVI (1959), 317–31. Primary sources on the Awakening are reprinted in Alan Heimert and Perry Miller (eds.), *The Great Awakening: Documents Illustrating the Crisis and Its Consequences* (Indianapolis, 1967); Richard L. Bushman (ed.), *The Great Awakening: Documents on the Revival of Religion, 1740–1745* (New York, 1970); and J. M. Bumsted (ed.), *The Great Awakening: The Beginnings of Evangelical Pietism in America* (Waltham, Mass., 1970). Darrett B. Rutman (ed.), *The Great Awakening: Event and Exegesis* (New York, 1970) contains documents plus interpretive essays. A general collection that contains essential materials on the church-state theme is J. F. Wilson (ed.), *Church and State in American History* (Boston, 1965).

For many individual states, there are now excellent studies of church-state relations in the late colonial period: for Virginia, George M. Brydon, *Virginia's Mother Church and the Political Conditions Under Which It Grew* (2 vols.; Philadelphia, 1952), supplemented by Rhys Issac, "Religion and Authority: Problems of the Anglican Establishment in Virginia in the Era of the Great Awakening and the Parsons' Cause," *William and Mary Quarterly*, 3d ser., XXX (1973), 3–36; for Maryland, A. W. Werline, *Problems of Church and State in Maryland During the Seventeenth and Eighteenth Centuries* (Lancaster, 1948); for Georgia, Reba C. Strickland, *Religion and the State in Georgia in the 18th Century* (New York, 1939); for New York, John W. Pratt, *Religion, Politics, and Divinity: The Church-State Theme in New York History* (Ithaca, 1967), chaps. 1–3; for Massachusetts, Jacob C. Meyer, *Church and State in Massachusetts, from 1740 to 1833* (Cleveland, 1930); for Connecticut, Sister Mary Paul Mason, *Church-State Relationships in Education in Connecticut, 1633–1953* (Washington, D.C., 1953), chap. 1; for New Hampshire, Charles B. Kinney, Jr., *Church and State: The Struggle for Separation in New Hampshire 1630–1900* (New York, 1955), chaps. 1–2. For New England, the starting point for any study of the development of separation of church and state is William G. McLoughlin, *New England Dissent, 1630–1833: The Baptists and the Separation of Church and State* (2 vols.; Cambridge, Mass. 1971)—a vast work of scholarship that obscures the importance of multiple establishment as a transitional stage from establishment to disestablishment, but which otherwise traces the separation theme most effectively.

The controversy over the meaning of the First Amendment has grown as a result of a series of Supreme Court cases on church-state questions related to education. The literature falls into two categories. The first, which might be called the "liberal interpretation," generally supports the direction the Court has taken in limiting the kind of support the state may render to parochial schools. Leading works are Leo Pfeffer, *Church, State and Freedom* (rev. ed.; Boston, 1967); R. Freeman Butts, *The American Tradition in Religion and Education* (Boston, 1950); Leonard W. Levy, "No Establishment of Religion: The Original Understanding" and "School Prayers and the Founding Fathers," in Levy, *Judgments: Essays on American Constitutional History* (Chicago, 1972); and Loren P. Beth, *The American Theory of Church and State* (Gainesville, Fla., 1958). The revisionist reaction to this interpretation has been distinguished and formidable, though, for me at least, not convincing. The most penetrating of these works is by the late eminent legal historian Mark DeWolfe Howe, *The Garden and the Wilderness: Religion and Government in American Constitutional History* (Chicago, 1965). See also Wilber G. Katz, *Religion and American Constitutions* (Evanston, Ill., 1963). A concentrated effort to rebut the liberal assessment of the original meaning of the First Amendment can be found in C. J. Antieau *et al., Freedom from Federal Establishment: Formation and Early History of the First Amendment Religion Clauses* (Milwaukee, 1964). Recent support for this view comes from one of the leading historians of American religion, William G. McLoughlin, in "The Role of Religion in the Revolution: Liberty of Conscience and Cultural Cohesion in the New Nation," in S. G. Kurtz and J. H. Hutson (eds.), *Essays on the American Revolution* (Chapel Hill, 1973).

Elwyn A. Smith's *Religious Liberty in the United States: The Development of Church-State Thought Since the Revolutionary Era* (Philadelphia, 1972), especially chaps. 4–6, helps to resolve these opposing positions by showing how religious thinkers ("republican theocrats") reconciled church-state separation and the perpetuation of religious values and institutions in the period after the adoption of the First Amendment. Carl Bridenbaugh's *Mitre and Sceptre: Transatlantic Faiths, Ideas, Personalities, and Politics, 1689–1775* (New York, 1962), reminds us of how real the threat of an Anglican establishment was in the period before the Revolution, and how the opposition to that threat helped to mold a "sense of American nationality" and a universal belief among Anglicans and dissenters alike that "in America there should be no union of church and state."

5. THE CONDITION OF THE PRESS

An early statement of the interpretive trend that emphasized the role of the legislature in press suppression was Harold Nelson's "Seditious Libel in Colonial America," *American Journal of Legislative History*, III (1959), 160–72. The best and most complete articulation and documentation of it, however, are the works of Leonard W. Levy: "Did the Zenger Case Really Matter?: Freedom of the Press in Colonial New York," *William and Mary Quarterly*, 3d ser., XVII (1960), 35–50; *Legacy of Suppression: Freedom of Speech and Press in Early American History* (Cambridge, Mass., 1960); and *Freedom of the Press from Zenger to Jefferson* (New York, 1966), a book of documents preceded by a long scholarly introduction. A concise and lucid account of the essential facts and legal points in the Zenger case can be found in Stanley N. Katz's modern edition of James Alexander's *A Brief Narrative of the Case and Trial of John Peter Zenger, Printer of the New York Weekly Journal* (Cambridge, Mass., 1963), especially pp. 1–35. For the role of James Alexander and the importance of Zenger's *journal* as opposed to Zenger's *trial*, see Vincent Buranelli, "Peter Zenger's Editor," *American Quarterly*, VII (1955), 174–81. The most complete catalogue of cases of press repression in the eighteenth century is in L. R. Schuyler, *The Liberty of the Press in the American Colonies Before the Revolutionary War* (New York, 1905). Daniel Boorstin's portrait of a conservative colonial press is presented in *The Americans: The Colonial Experience* (New York, 1958), chap. 51.

A challenge to the Levy school is made in Lawrence H. Leder's

Liberty and Authority: Early American Political Ideology, 1689–1769 (Chicago, 1968), much of which is based on pamphlet, broadside, magazine, and newspaper evidence—a book that rests upon the fundamental assumption that the colonial press reflected a wide range of opinion on basic political and constitutional issues. In Chapter 1, Leder contends that, if freedom of the press was not yet defined clearly in law, it certainly was appreciated and exercised in practice. Writers increasingly understood the relationship between free press and free government. Leder's findings were first published in "The Role of Newspapers in Early America: 'In Defense of Their Own Liberty,'" *Huntington Library Quarterly*, XXX (1966), 1–16. James M. Smith also criticizes the Levy interpretation in his review of *Legacy of Suppression* in the *William and Mary Quarterly*, 3d ser., XX (1963), 156–59.

The economic aspects of the printing trade are analyzed in interesting detail by Peter J. Parker in "The Philadelphia Printer: A Study of an 18th Century Businessman," *Business History Review*, XL (1966), 24–26. Lawrence C. Wroth's classic, *The Colonial Printer* (Portland, 1938), is particularly strong on the technical aspects of printing in the period. The problems of news-gathering are also discussed in the useful text by Frank L. Mott, *American Journalism: A History, 1690–1960* (3d ed.; New York, 1962). Valuable for its encyclopedic character is Douglas C. McMurtrie's *A History of Printing in the United States* (New York, 1936), the modern successor to Isaiah Thomas's *History of Printing in America* (2 vols., Worcester, Mass., 1810).

Richard L. Merritt's application of new methodology has revealed how important the colonial press was both as mirror and as shaper of a rising "American" consciousness. See his "Public Opinion in Colonial America: Content Analyzing the Colonial Press," in *Public Opinion Quarterly* (1963), 356–71, and *Symbols of American Community, 1735–1775* (New Haven, Conn., 1965). For the role of the press in the crisis of the Revolution, see Philip Davidson, *Propaganda and the American Revolution, 1763–1783* (Chapel Hill, 1941), and Arthur M. Schlesinger, Sr., *Prelude to Independence: The Newspaper War on Great Britain, 1764–1776* (New York, 1958).

Useful material on individual printers, newspapers, and magazines can be found in L. N. Richardson, *A History of Early Magazines, 1741–1789* (New York, 1931); P. L. Ford (ed.), *The Journals of Hugh Gaine, Printer* (2 vols.; New York, 1902); Anna J. De Armond, *Andrew Bradford, Colonial Journalist* (Newark, Del., 1949); and Hennig Cohen, *The South Carolina Gazette, 1732–1775* (Columbia, S.C., 1953)—as well as in the general studies previously cited. Of special value for its material on New York's press in the 1950's is the modern edition of *The Independent Reflector* . . . (Cambridge, Mass., 1963), ed. by Milton M. Klein. For an example of a confrontation between an editor and an assembly, see Beverly McAnear, "James Parker Versus New York Province," *New York History*, XXII (1941), 321–30. On the McDougall controversy in New York, see D. R. Dillon, *The New York Triumvirate* . . . (New York, 1949), chap. 6.

The only biography of William Smith, provost of the Philadelphia College, is Albert F. Gegenheimer's *William Smith: Educator and Churchman, 1727–1803* (Philadelphia, 1943). For Smith's fluctuating relationship with Benjamin Franklin, the leader of Philadelphia life and society, see Ralph L. Ketcham, "Benjamin Franklin and William Smith: New Light on an Old Philadelphia Quarrel," *Pennsylvania Magazine of History and Biography*, LXXXVIII (1964), 142–63. On the political issues surrounding Pennsylvania's participation in the French and Indian Wars, see Ketcham's "Conscience, War, and Politics in Pennsylvania, 1755–1757," *William and Mary Quarterly*, 3d ser., XX (1963), 416–39; for Franklin's role also consult William S. Hanna, *Benjamin Franklin and Pennsylvania Politics* (Stanford, 1964). More general treatments of Pennsylvania politics during this whole period are Dietmar Rothermund, *The Layman's Progress: Religious and Political Experience in Colonial Pennsylvania, 1740–1770* (Philadelphia, 1961), and J. H. Hutson, *Pennsylvania Politics: The Movement for Royal Government and Its Consequences* (Princeton, 1972). Richard Bauman examines the changing political attitudes and behavior of the Pennsylvania Quakers during this period in *For the Reputation of Truth: Politics, Religion, and Conflict Among the Pennsylvania Quakers, 1750–1800* (Baltimore, 1971).

The confrontation between the governor (acting for Thomas

Penn, the proprietor) and the assembly during the period of the Smith-Moore controversy is analyzed by Nicholas B. Wainwright in "Governor William Denny in Pennsylvania," *Pennsylvania Magazine of History*, LXXXI (1957), 170–98. The fullest account of the legal questions at issue in the case of Smith and Moore can be found in the lengthy "Libel in the Assembly: A Pre-Revolutionary Episode," *Pennsylvania Magazine of History*, LII (1928), 176–92, 249–79, 342–60.

6. The Character of Politics

Most of the important recent work on colonial political life has been done on a colony-by-colony basis. A few excellent general treatments, however, are available. Bernard Bailyn's *Origins of American Politics* (New York, 1968) establishes the ideological context in which colonial politics can be understood, but it also details the political situation in the provinces in the pre-Revolutionary period. Useful for its comparison of political life in England and America is J. R. Pole's *Political Representation in England and the Origins of the American Republic* (New York, 1966). For a penetrating survey of the recent work and an analysis of its import and thrust, see Jack P. Greene, "Changing Interpretations of Early American Politics," in R. A. Billington (ed.), *The Reinterpretation of Early American History: Essays in Honor of John E. Pomfret* (San Marino, 1966), 151–84.

There are a number of excellent modern studies of suffrage, voting practices, and legislative apportionment in the various colonies. For New Jersey, see Richard P. McCormick, *The History of Voting in New Jersey: A Study of the Development of Election Machinery, 1664–1911* (New Brunswick, 1953), chaps. 1–2; Robert H. Rich, "Election Machinery in New Jersey, 1702–1775," *N.J. Hist. Soc. Proc.*, LXVII (1949), 198–217; and J. R. Pole, "Suffrage Reform and the American Revolution in New Jersey," *N.J. Hist. Soc. Proc.*, LXXIV (1956), 173–94. For Massachusetts, see Robert E. Brown, "Democracy in Colonial Massachusetts," *New England Quarterly*, XXV (1952), 291–313, and *Middle-Class Democracy and the Revolution in Massachusetts, 1691–1780* (Ithaca, 1955); and J. R. Pole, "Suffrage and Representation in Massachusetts: A Statistical Note," *William and Mary Quarterly*, 3d ser., XIV (1957), 560–92. For Plymouth, which was eventually absorbed by Massachusetts, see George D. Langdon, Jr., "The Franchise and Political Democracy in Plymouth," *William and Mary Quarterly*, XX (1963), 513–26. For New York, see Milton M. Klein, "Democracy and Politics in Colonial New York," *New York History*, XL (1959), 221–46; and Nicholas Varga, "Election Procedures and Practices in Colonial New York," *New York History*, XLI (1960), 249–77. For Virginia, see Charles S. Sydnor, *American Revolutionaries in the Making: Political Practices in Washington's Virginia* (2d ed.; New York, 1965); and R. E. Brown and B. K. Brown, *Virginia, 1705–1786: Democracy or Aristocracy?* (East Lansing, 1964), chaps. 6 and 7. For Pennsylvania, see Sister Joan de Lourdes Leonard, C.S.J., "Elections in Colonial Pennsylvania," *William and Mary Quarterly*, 3d ser., XI (1954), 385–401; and Norman S. Cohen, "The Philadelphia Election Riot of 1742," *Pennsylvania Magazine of History and Biography*, XCII (1968), 306–19. The most comprehensive work is Chilton Williamson, *American Suffrage: From Property to Democracy, 1760–1860* (Princeton, 1960), chaps. 1–3.

A number of works not primarily concerned with the question of voting include interesting and useful information on the subject nevertheless. A few examples are David S. Lovejoy, *Rhode Island Politics and the American Revolution, 1760–1776* (Providence, 1958); Lucille Griffith, *The Virginia House of Burgesses, 1750–1774* (rev. ed.; University, Ala., 1968); and Patricia U. Bonomi, *A Factious People: Politics and Society in Colonial New York* (New York, 1971).

For leading examples of the literature critical of the "democratic" explanation of colonial politics, see Roy N. Lokken, "The Concept of Democracy in Colonial Political Thought," *William and Mary Quarterly*, XVI (1959), 568–80, which shows that the concept of democracy was rooted in classical thought and had a very circumscribed meaning in the colonial period. J. R. Pole, in "Historians and the Problem of Early American Democracy," *American Historical Review*, LXVII (1962), 626–46, argues that colonial society was "deferential" rather than "democratic." In "Democracy and the American Revolution: A Frame of Reference," *William and Mary Quarterly*, XXI (1964), 165–90, Richard Buel, Jr., emphasizes the importance of the representative assembly as a kind of arbiter between the rulers and the ruled and explains that voters had little opportunity to initiate policy and only enough power to keep their elected representatives in check. In "The Myths of Colonial Democracy and Royal Decline in 18th Century America: A Review Essay," *Cithara*, V (1965), 53–69, John Murrin vigorously attacks the logic of the Browns in their book on Virginia and shows how their evidence can be used to explain the existence of aristocracy as much as democracy. Michael Zuckerman argues that, on the local level, consensus rather than democratic majoritarianism was the purpose of extending the franchise as widely as possible; see his "The Social Context of Democracy in Massachusetts," *William and Mary Quarterly*, 3d. ser., XXV (1968), 523–44.

The text account of the Land Bank controversy in Massachusetts is based upon George A. Billias, "The Massachusetts Land Bankers of 1740," *University of Maine Bulletin*, LXI (1959), which refutes the traditional debtor-creditor split over this financial scheme; and Robert Zemsky, *Merchants, Farmers, and River Gods: An Essay on 18th Century American Politics* (Boston, 1971), chaps. 5–6. A helpful introduction to the problem of colonial finance is E. James Ferguson, "Currency Finance: An Interpretation of Monetary Practices," *William and Mary Quarterly*, 3d ser., X (1953), 153–80. On the wide use of land bank measures in other colonies, see Theodore Thayer, "The Land Bank System in the American Colonies," *Journal of Economic History*, XIII (1953), 145–59.

To compare the divergent English and American concepts of the representative function, consult J. R. Pole, *The 17th Century: The Sources of Legislative Power* (Charlottesville, 1969), for the origins, and Bernard Bailyn, *The Ideological Origins of the American Revolution* (Cambridge, 1967), chap. 5, for the mid-eighteenth-century view. Gordon S. Wood, in *The Creation of the American Republic, 1776–1787* (Chapel Hill, 1969), traces the shift in, and clarification of, American thinking on the subject in the period from the Revolution to the Constitution.

My discussion of political faction in colonial society draws upon Greene, "Changing Interpretations," and Bailyn, *Origins of American Politics*, chaps. 2–3. Altogether, Bailyn discovered four examples reflective of the new conception of politics discussed in the text. My own research uncovered two more examples—those from Zenger's *Weekly Journal* and Smith's *American Magazine*. A thorough survey of the colonial press in this period should reveal still more support for the Bailyn thesis that I am following. For further discussion of the evolution of the notion of party, see Richard Hofstadter, *The Idea of a Party System: The Rise of Legitimate Opposition in the United States, 1780–1840* (Berkeley, 1969). The phrase a "Constitution against parties" is the title of chapter 2 of that work.

An early example of the new historiographical trend which has emphasized the role of faction in colonial politics is Oscar Zeichner's *Connecticut's Years of Controversy, 1750–1776* (Chapel Hill, 1949). Patricia U. Bonomi sees in the faction real signs of political maturity. Her important book, *A Factious People,* is representative of the growing trend whose thrust rejects earlier notions, based on eighteenth-century judgments, that faction betokened lack of political development. Stanley N. Katz's *Newcastle's New York: Anglo-American Politics, 1732–1753* (Cambridge, Mass., 1968), sheds much light on a number of the themes considered in the text.

Index

Academy and Charitable School (Philadelphia), 118
Act of Settlement (1701) and judicial independence, 46
Act of Toleration (1689), 80, 83. *See also* Freedom of conscience; Toleration
Acts of Trade. *See* Navigation Acts
Adams, John, 139
Admiralty, 27
Age of Enlightenment, 73, 88
Alexander, James, 109, 113, 148
American Magazine and Monthly Chronicle for the British Colonies, 121, 123–27, 151–52
American Revolution: and assembly development, 156; and church establishments, 92, 93, 95, 99, 101, 104, 105, 107; and governmental structures, 51–52; legislators' function defined, 142; and politics, 152; and press, 114, 125–26; and property rights, 143; and republicanism, 104; and transfer of common law, 53, 57, 63, 75
Anglicans and Anglican Church: American bishop, 120; location, 85–87; in particular colonies, 79, 81, 92, 94–96, 98, 99, 100, 114

Assemblies (colonial): compared with Parliament, 39, 44, 143; conflict over judiciary and, 46–47; in particular colonies, 83, 119–26, 138–40; and politics, 145–47, 155; and press, 117–18, 121–28; purposes, functions, and powers of, 36–44, 144, 152; in relation to councils, 43, 139; in relation to governors, 42–43, 139–40, 145. *See also* Councils; Courts of justice; Governors; Legislatures
Arminianism, 88

Bailyn, Bernard, 37, 141, 144, 145
Baptists: location in general, 85–87; in particular colonies, 94, 95, 96, 98, 100; and church-state separation, 102, 104
Belcher, Jonathan, 138, 139
Bellomont, Earl of, 33
Bicameralism, in Massachusetts, 39–40
Billias, George A., 140
Blackstone, Sir William, 42, 57, 71–72, 109
Bloodless Revolution (1688–89): and emergence of toleration, 80; and Parliamentary power, 27, 41–42